SET-UP REDUCTION

Saving Dollars with Common Sense

SET-UP REDUCTION

Saving Dollars with Common Sense

JERRY W. CLAUNCH

PHILIP D. STANG

with a Foreword by
PETER L. GRIECO, JR.
and
MICHAEL W. GOZZO

PT PUBLICATIONS, INC.
4360 NORTH LAKE BLVD.
PALM BEACH GARDENS, FL 33410
(407) 624-0455

Library of Congress Cataloging in Publication Data

Claunch, Jerry W., 1947-
  Set-up reduction: saving dollars with common sense / Jerry W.
Claunch, Philip D. Stang.
  Bibliography;
  Includes index.
  1. Assembly-line methods 2. Production management. I. Stang,
Philip D., 1946- . II. Title.
TS178.4.C58   1990
658.5 ' 1—dc20

                                        89-27627
                                        CIP

ISBN 0-945456-04-2

To my father
who instilled in me
a mechanical aptitude.
To Sandy for the time
this took and the continuous
encouragement she gives me.
Jerry W. Claunch

To Dianne
My inspiration,
My strength,
My best friend,
My wife.
Always
Phil Stang

TABLE OF CONTENTS

FOREWORD

As this book was being developed and reviewed, we began to reflect upon the state of manufacturing. There is much of which we should be proud, however, there is much which we still need to do. Our competition is already progressing in areas where many of our companies are just starting. For instance, many Japanese companies have an extremely organized customer and supplier network. Instead of dealing directly with every potential customer and supplier, their objective is to deal only with customers and suppliers that can merge the concept and philosophy of Just-In-Time. They only want to do business with suppliers that are flexible and can quickly change over their manufacturing process in order to meet the demands of customers.

Japanese customers know they can rely on all their suppliers to get material to the manufacturing plant on time, 100 percent of the time. And this is possible because Japanese companies like Toyota have first stressed quality and set-up reduction internally, that is, in their own plants. They have sought suppliers who are willing to strive for set-up reduction. Set-up reduction at Japanese companies is both an internal and external program. Suppliers drive their trucks directly into the inner reaches of the Toyota plant and unload their shipments right at the work center, often within 10 feet of the production line. As the delivery is unloaded, the parts are immediately put into production without long set-ups. Four hours later, another shipment arrives. Needless to say, only a company capable of small lot sizes and very short set-up times can be flexible enough to meet this exacting schedule of customer demand.

We realized the challenge we must meet on a recent trip through the Toyota Plant as we watched supplier's parts being delivered on time in the correct quantities. That challenge, as Jerry and Phil state it in this book, is that *the best set-up is no set-up at all.* We recommend that you remember this principle as you begin to implement your own set-up reduction program.

Another purpose of this book is to stress the relationship between reduction of set-up time, the reduction of lot sizes and inventory reduction so that companies can become more flexible, more responsive to customer demand. It does not take a prophet to see that the global marketplace will demand this level of World Class Excellence in the 1990s and beyond.

SET-UP TIME AND LOT SIZES

Set-up time is the amount of time it takes to change over a work center from the production of one item of 100% quality to another item of 100% quality. It is measured from the point where the last good product of item A was produced to the first good product of item B is made at normal efficiency. The intent of set-up reduction is to reduce production set-up times in order to support a movement toward small lot sizes, lower levels of inventory and improvements in productivity.

The ideal manufacturing objective is to perform set-ups so quickly that lot sizes of one can be accomplished. To obtain levels approaching that ideal requires a persistent effort on one machine at a time, a Continuous Improvement Process (CIP).

SET-UP REDUCTION GOALS

The goal is zero. The theoretical goal of a set-up reduction program is to eliminate the requirement for set-up entirely.

The 50 percent rule. The first step is to reduce set-up time by at least 50 percent. Then, the lot size and inventory should also be reduced by 50 percent and a new 50 percent set-up reduction goal established. This process will insure the maximum controlled benefits from the program and deliver a maximum return on investment.

Low-Cost/No-Cost. There should be a minimum of a 50 percent reduction in set-up time with a low-cost/no-cost solution. Set-up reduction and its inherent efficiencies are an integral component of the the drive to be the low-cost producer. Reductions in set-up need not only explore the most expensive or hi-tech solutions, but should explore a more simple solution which adds little or no cost.

PEOPLE ISSUES

Set-up reduction is not a program to eliminate the set-up people. The objective is to reduce set-up time to as close to zero as possible, so that the set-up person can change over a machine as many times a day as required by customer demand.

When changes are proposed, the question most asked by workers is "What's in it for me?" This is why this book stresses involving them in teams. Teams should be given the responsibility and authority to challenge everything in order to fund the future today. Nothing, not one procedure is sacred. Growth, improvement, cost reduction only comes when you begin challenging accepted practices. Now the challenge is yours: To reduce set-up time and lot sizes so that you can become World Class *TODAY!*

Peter L. Grieco, Jr.
Michael W. Gozzo

West Palm Beach, Florida

ACKNOWLEDGEMENTS

We wish to thank our clients and the people who have attended our Set-Up Reduction programs throughout the world for their active support and examples. Equally important have been the interactions with some of our consulting staff: Chip Long, Mel Pilachowski, Wayne Douchkoff, Paul Hine and Frank Ford. We thank them for their examples, anecdotes and suggestions.

In particular, we would like to thank Peter L. Grieco, Jr., and Michael W. Gozzo, co-founders of Professionals for Technology Associates, Inc., for their long and continuous support and for writing the Foreword. We wish them success on the publication of their forthcoming books on Negotiation and Employee Involvement.

Another pillar of support has been provided by our capable office staff of Rita Grieco, Leslie Echelson, Dawn Souby, Theresa Spingola and Collen Poole. Special thanks are due to Kevin Grieco for the art work which he created to explain key concepts.

As always, we would like to express our continued appreciation to a major member of the team, Steven Marks, for his editorial assistance in preparing yet another book in a series which covers today's most urgent manufacturing problems and their solutions.

We hope that your reading will be as pleasurable as our efforts.

SET-UP REDUCTION

Saving Dollars
with Common Sense

CHAPTER ONE

FUNDING THE FUTURE

Something is happening in American manufacturing and it is quietly revolutionizing the way we build products. It's time that the secret be finally uncovered so that we can all benefit from the dramatic results these innovators in manufacturing are obtaining. What are these results which would astound most manufacturers? Consider the following:

> • **A company reduces the set-up time on a production line from eight hours to two minutes.**

- **Another company cuts its lot sizes in half and reduces its inventory carrying costs by over 25 percent.**

- **Still another company is able to produce all 15 flavors of its product in the same day, on the same machine, in exactly the quantities required by its customers.**

Where, you are probably asking yourself, are these companies? In the Far East? No, they are all here in America and they are the beginning of a groundswell called set-up reduction, or quick changeover.

Companies on the leading edge of manufacturing technology are finding that set-up reduction is the wave which they will ride into the future. Like a surfer who has caught the most powerful part of the wave, these companies are outpacing their competition. Set-up reduction allows companies to unlock hidden capacity and to increase productivity while drastically lowering total cost. This allows them to increase profits and to take advantage of market share.

There are, of course, obstacles. Neither surfing nor set-up reduction is easy, but, with education and application, any obstacles can be overcome. How to implement a successful set-up reduction program in your company which turns these obstacles into opportunities is what this book is about. Although set-up reduction is hard work, we can help you avoid falling off your surfboard. The trick to maintaining your balance as you set out to implement your own program is to remember that set-up reduction is based on a

Total Business Concept (TBC). By this, we mean that you cannot reach the shore of success unless you are aware of all the forces and factors which affect your ride on the leading edge of the wave. Most failures result from a company failing to see that set-up reduction is part of an overall and company-wide commitment to eliminate waste and a dedication to the continuous improvement process.

Set-up reduction is not just about replacing nuts and bolts with quick disconnects. The technical details are certainly a vital part of set-up reduction, but you cannot expect equipment and tooling changes alone to have any significant impact. Set-up reduction is not set-up reduction unless it includes lot sizing, Zero Inventory (ZI), Just-In-Time (JIT), Total Quality Control (TQC), Preventive Maintenance (PM), Total Cost Management (TCM) and many other areas which encompass the world class manufacturing mind-set. To be on the leading edge of manufacturing means that we will have to understand how set-up reduction relates to all areas of the company. People in the company will have to see the larger picture as well. Anything less than starting with a total education and training program is like putting a pair of blinders on a surfer. How is he supposed to see the right wave, the hidden rocks, the dock pilings, the other surfers or the ever-present competition?

The first question to ask yourself is whether a company culture puts blinders on its people. Are people ready for problems to surface so that they can solve them or are they afraid for them to surface? Our people won't follow us if we are afraid or unable to lead or to uncover old or traditional practices which are detrimental to our future progress. North American manufacturers need to emerge once again as the leaders in manufacturing. We can if we squarely face the problems before us. Every problem is an opportunity in disguise. Let's start setting a pattern for improvement by reducing set-up *NOW*.

WHY REDUCE SET-UP?

We have found in our dealings in the United States, Canada and Europe that, given some gentle prodding, most people want to reduce set-up, but don't know how. In fact, over the years, we have developed a list of key motivations for addressing the issue of set-up reduction. Many of the items are topics being discussed in your company today.

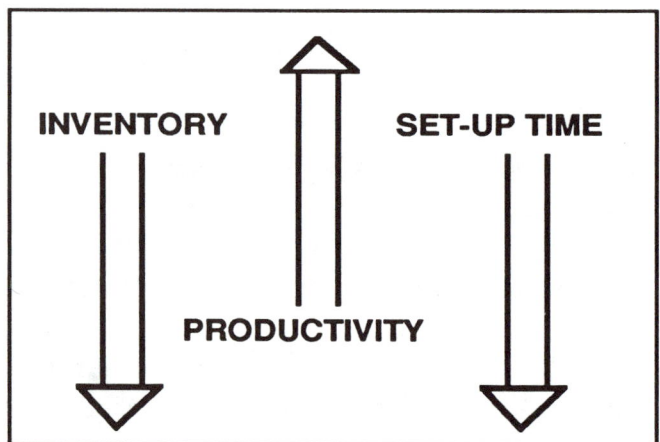

REDUCE COSTS— There are three principal costs incurred by a company—material, employee (labor) and equipment costs. A set-up reduction program will lower inventories and therefore lower the cost of carrying inventory. In the long run, it will lower employee set-up time and allow them to be more productive by freeing up operators to perform other tasks such as maintenance and continuous improvement in quality and lowest total cost. (It should be mentioned here that set-up reduction is not a program to replace or reduce the number of employees. If management is not committed to this, your program will fail.) Set-up reduction also lowers machine cost by increasing the machine's productivity.

REDUCE LOT SIZES—Many companies have attempted to cut lot sizes without addressing set-up reduction. This will guarantee an increase in the set-up cost per unit and erode credibility in the lot size reduction strategy. It is a lot like throwing out the parachute first and hoping you can catch it!

REDUCE LEAD TIME—Lead time consists of five elements—queue, set-up, run, wait and move. Since set-up reduction enables you to reduce lot sizes, you will find that the frequency of product runs will increase and that the amount of material in queue will also be greatly reduced. And, since queue time is usually the largest element of lead time, you can expect to see the lead time for the manufacturing of a product decrease dramatically. This is also a major element of waste in an organization.

REDUCE INVENTORY—The philosophy of Just-In-Time results in lower inventory. Set-up reduction is, in fact, a driver of this philosophy which results in inventory reduction. It also has an effect which extends beyond its particular area. As mentioned before, set-up reduction reduces lot sizes and, thus, the need to carry safety stock as a hedge against long lead times. The average on-hand inventory and associated carrying costs are reduced correspondingly. Therefore, inventory reduction is a key result of any set-up reduction program.

INCREASE CAPACITY—In most manufacturing environments, companies are up against the constraints of their resources of money, equipment and manpower. Set-up reduction introduces a level of flexibility which allows companies to tap the capacity of all these areas to their fullest or, more precisely, to schedule the use of these resources based on customer demand. When a company can change its equipment over in minutes versus hours, the result is a capacity increase. Capacity increases of 25 percent are not uncommon in a set-up reduction program.

INCREASE FLEXIBILITY—Whether your company is a job shop, a continuous or a repetitive manufacturer, set-up reduction increases your flexibility to manufacture products to demand. This is possible simply because it takes less time to change from the production of one item to another. Whereas once it was only possible to run Item A once a week because the set-up took one day to complete, now the same item can be run many times a day along with Item B, Item C, etc. When set-up times are counted in terms of minutes (and sometimes seconds) instead of hours and days, it is clear you can change over more often.

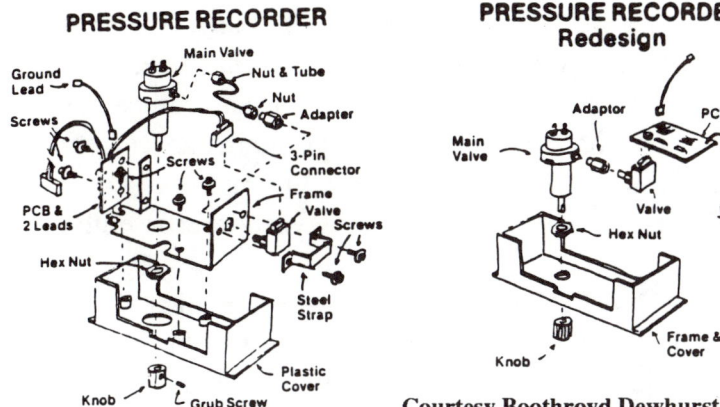

PRESSURE RECORDER

Main Valve
Ground Lead
Nut & Tube
Nut
Adapter
Screws
Screws
3-Pin Connector
Frame
PCB & 2 Leads
Valve
Screws
Hex Nut
Steel Strap
Plastic Cover
Knob
Grub Screw

**PRESSURE RECORDER
Redesign**

Adaptor
PCB & 1 Lead
Main Valve
Valve
Hex Nut
Frame & Cover
Knob

Courtesy Boothroyd Dewhurst, Inc.

IMPROVE TOOL AND PRODUCT DESIGN—One of the infrequently mentioned benefits of set-up reduction is the improvement in tool and product design which results from teams consisting of design, marketing and manufacturing staffs working together. When these departments set out to solve problems collectively, you will avoid the "over the wall" syndrome which plagues so many companies. In this situation, for example, engineering designs a product and then throws their plan over the wall to the production department with no consideration of the producibility of the item. The real issue at hand is to design a product or tool with quick changeover in mind.

IDLE ASSETS—Whether the assets are manpower, capital, facility or equipment, set-up reduction demands that you build only what you sell. Thus, there should be no finished goods inventory stored in warehouses accruing carrying costs. The old financial rule says that we should keep all assets busy. The new manufacturing rule says that we run machines only when we have a customer demand. Many companies find that with a set-up reduction program they can expand their business without needing more space or other assets. They use what they have more efficiently.

INCREASE PRODUCTIVITY—Companies have talked about increasing productivity for the last 50 years, just as they have talked about quality. Everybody wants to improve, but, in fact, productivity for most industries in the United States has stood still since 1973. Set-up reduction will increase your ability to produce. It will increase your productivity because you will be making products that are in demand by customers. The goal of set-up reduction is not to keep people and machines busy producing goods which are stored in warehouses. The warehousing of unwanted goods has been described as "nothing more than transportation at zero velocity!"

IMPROVE QUALITY—A set-up reduction program is not only a process which reduces the time it takes to perform a set-up. The process also looks for creative ways to set up machines so that they produce parts right the first time. Such an approach automatically improves quality because it is process oriented. Quality is built into the set-up process. In addition, smaller lot sizes reduce the exposure to quality problems encountered within a specific batch. If you manufacture 5,000 pieces, there are 5,000 potential defective parts. If, however, you have reduced the lot size in half because of your set-up program, there are now only 2,500 potential defective parts. A lot size of one, of course, would result in only one potential defect.

REDUCE SCRAP—Set-up reduction demands that a company make parts right the first time. This means no more rework and rejects since the measurement of set-up time is from the last good part to the next good part produced at normal efficiency rate.

HAPPY CUSTOMERS—A happy customer is different from a satisfied customer. A happy customer gets what he or she wants when they want it. A set-up reduction program enables you to manufacture 100 percent quality parts which are shipped on time, all the time, to the customer in the exact quantities requested.

HAPPY EMPLOYEES—It is not only the simplification of set-up operations which will improve employee job satisfaction. Far more important is the new sense of teamwork which will result from people joining together to solve real problems creatively. At first, there may be resistance to the set-up program. Fear of job security is a real factor, but it will ultimately disappear when employees see the results start to come in.

REDUCE OVERTIME—Companies often make the

mistake of assuming that employees want overtime. In our experience, we have found that many employees would rather spend the time with their family or pursuing their own outside interests. We suggest that you develop a policy in which some of the savings generated by set-up reduction are given back to the employees as an incentive to make further gains.

IMPROVE MATERIAL FLOW—Set-up reduction, by virtue of its reduction in lot sizes and inventory, requires less inventory to keep the material flowing at a productive rate. The less inventory you have, the less you have to control and the easier and less costly the job of material management becomes.

INCREASE MAINTENANCE TIME—The less time required for a set-up, the less components or material required for a manufacturing run. The increased flexibility which results from smaller lot sizes allows more time to perform scheduled preventive maintenance.

THE BENEFITS OF SET-UP REDUCTION

With a little twist, most of the above motivators result in benefits for the company. However, we will never know just how beneficial the far-reaching effects of set-up reduction are unless we establish measurements to gauge progress. A discussion of these performance measurements are in a later chapter. For now, as you read the benefits on the next page, start addressing ways to track these benefits in your own company right from the start.

SET-UP REDUCTION
BENEFITS FOR YOUR COMPANY

- Become more competitive.
- Become more profitable.
- Experience fewer shortages or stock-outs.
- Increase uptime of equipment; machines are available and ready to run.
- Improve cash flow.
- Reduce queue time; on the average, 75-80 percent of lead time is queue time, time in which work is actually sitting still.
- Reduce inventory, including purchased material, work-in-process (WIP) and finished goods. All inventory eats up enormous amounts of profit.
- Improve management and supervision by increasing flexibility; managers and supervisors can concentrate on their duties, instead of putting out fires.
- Improve inventory turns; either by increasing sales or by reducing inventory through a set-up program.
- Reduce indirect costs.
- Improve customer service.
- Lower lot sizes.
- Improve machine efficiency and level out production schedules.
- Utilize labor more efficiently.
- Increase manufacturing flexibility and capability.

There is one benefit which requires further discussion. This benefit is the reduction of waste. Waste is defined as:

> **Anything other than**
> **the absolute minimum resources**
> **of material, machines**
> **and manpower required**
> **to add value to the product.**

The seven categories of waste in the area of set-up reduction are listed in the box on the following page. Set-up reduction's goal is to involve employees in the elimination of waste by a process which results in no wasted time and labor and no scrap parts.

SET-UP REDUCTION GOALS

THE GOAL IS ZERO.

The theoretical goal of set-up reduction is to eliminate entirely the need to perform a set-up. This is normally attained only through the use of dedicated equipment, that is, machines which only make one part. Striving to reach the goal of zero drives the Continuous Improvement Process (CIP).

THE 50 PERCENT RULE.

The minimum increment for a "targeted" set-up reduction is 50 percent. In other words, a goal of a 50 percent decrease in set-up time is matched by a 50 percent reduction in lot size. When this is

CATEGORY	WHY (EXCUSE)
OVERPRODUCING Companies often produce something for which there is no market or customer. The result is increased obsolete inventory and carrying costs.	**Producing to keep people busy.**
QUEUE Time spent waiting for real work to be done.	**Large lot sizes.**
TRANSPORTATION Less costly for companies to ship more frequently and in smaller quantities.	**Lack of traffic coordinator or a logistics function.**
INVENTORY High level of excess or obsolete inventory.	**EOQ formula presently drives process.**
UNNECESSARY MOTION Set-up reduction eliminates awkward steps and combines motions.	**"The way we were" or "That's the way we used to do it."**
PRODUCING DEFECTIVE GOODS "Make it right the first time!"	**2% AQL factor.**
SET-UP TIME Necessary in today's business to counteract the traditional method of increasing machine time and driving up lot sizes which result in increased inventory and wasted labor.	**EOQ formula and cost rules about absorption.**

achieved, then you set a new 50 percent set-up reduction goal. Once the new set-up goal is met, reduce the lot size again by 50 percent. Later, you will see how this dramatically reduces inventory levels with no danger of running out of material.

THE LOW COST/NO COST SOLUTION.

We have been able to prove to companies that they can attain a 75 percent reduction in set-up time with a low cost/ no cost solution. Reductions in set-up time need not incorporate expensive, hi-tech solutions. The best approach is to simplify the operations which comprise a set-up. We also tell companies that they cannot buy set-up reduction. It's not for sale. They may have to invest some money in training or in some new tools, but they are not going to buy set-up reduction without investing in creative energy.

If you are wondering just how much money may need to be invested, consider the following examples we have encountered. One team recently needed $1,500 to reduce a set-up. Would you have provided the funds? Would you have given it to them if you had known that this investment saved the company $50,000 in the first year? A set-up team at another client needed $100,000. Would you have invested that much money if you could be sure of a savings of $2.4 million? This client was only too happy to have made that investment.

A typical cost benefit graph for implementing set-up reduction looks like the one on the following page. As you can see, the benefits do begin to accrue. This graph, by the way, often serves to muffle any criticism of a set-up reduction program. When upper management sees what their company has achieved, they are more apt to become advocates of set-up reduction themselves and press for more results.

PRODUCTIVITY

There is one other point to be made with regard to the cost benefits

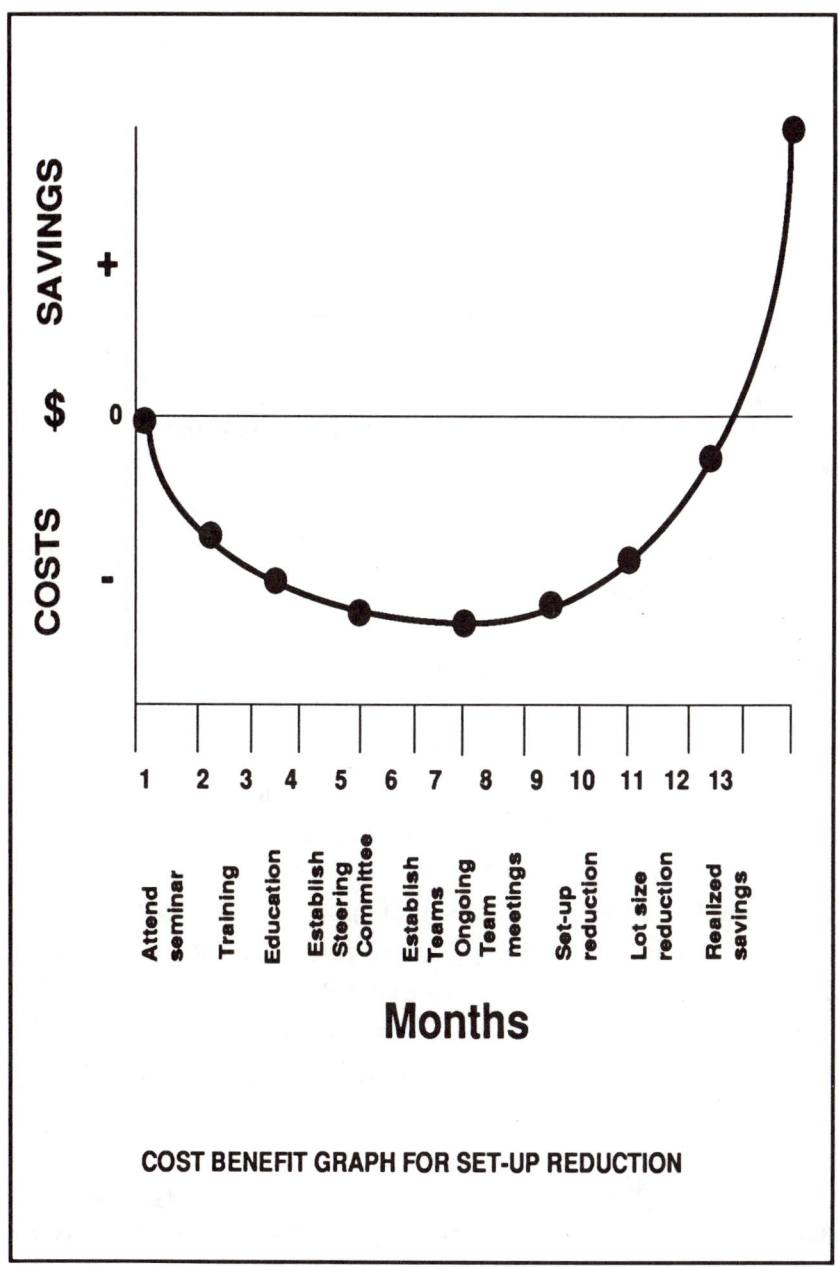

COST BENEFIT GRAPH FOR SET-UP REDUCTION

of set-up reduction and productivity. The formula for productivity is:

$$\text{PRODUCTIVITY} = \frac{\text{OUTPUT}}{\text{INPUT}}$$

Companies traditionally use this formula any time they are making parts. But, are output and input alone an accurate reflection of a company's productivity? We believe, as Kaplan and Johnson do in their book, *Relevance Lost*, that productivity must be based on Total Cost. Later in this book, we will discuss this in more detail and how it relates to set-up reduction. Today, we must understand that in a total cost environment, the productivity formula must be interpreted differently.

For example, is a company being productive when it produces parts for which there is no present customer demand? Is it a true reflection of productivity if the cost of storing these parts is not factored into the formula? A total cost interpretation of the productivity formula defines output as products built to customer demand and input is defined as all the costs associated with the production of goods. Total cost management is the true measurement of efficiency, unlike purchase price variance (PPV), machine up-time, etc. It is the measurement of how close companies come to lot-for-lot production, that is, how close they come to the building, shipping, invoicing and receiving payment for only what a customer ordered each day.

The goal is to produce today what you sold yesterday in order to avoid paying the cost of carrying inventory which, in most industries, ranges between 25 and 30 percent of product cost. That means a savings between $250,000 and $300,000 on every $1 million worth of inventory your company holds. Set-up reduction will help you realize those savings immediately.

RELATIONSHIP
TO INVENTORY MANAGEMENT

The goal of set-up reduction is to manufacture in one day all the items you need in order to fill customer orders and not to build in anticipation. This is possible if the set-up time is fast enough to allow the rapid changeover from one product line to another or one part to another. The direct result of this "pull" system of production in which set-up times are greatly reduced is a significant reduction in inventory as well as no more stock-outs.

Before we show you how to achieve this, we must first look at the traditional sawtooth curve of inventory management. Let's assume for all the following examples that it takes 3 weeks to replace inventory and that you use 4 parts per week. Let's also assume that we begin with 100 parts. Given these conditions, your reorder point should be 12. It should be a simple matter then for you to order 100 more parts whenever your inventory falls to 12, or every 22 weeks. And without fail, you are going to order 100 parts and receive them 3 weeks later, just as your inventory drops to zero. Right? Just like the graph on the top of the next page.

Suppliers (internal or external) are never late, are they? Your production levels never deviate because of fluctuations in demand

Set-Up Reduction

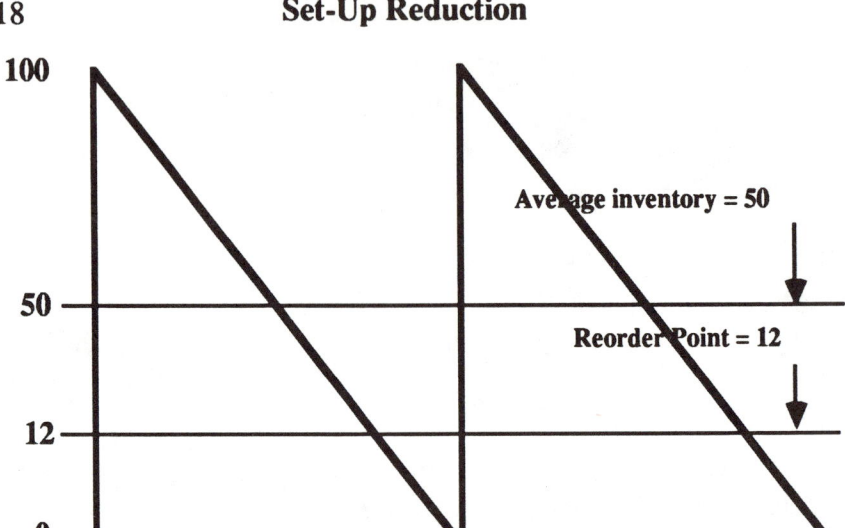

Traditional Sawtooth Curve

either. Right? As you are probably only too aware, the one thing we can all count on is that things change. Murphy's Law applies throughout the universe, so, to be safe, you add a safety stock of 10 parts. Instead of JIT (Just-In-Time), you now have JIC (Just-In-Case). On a graph, JIC inventory management looks like the illustration on the following page.

By adding safety stock, however, your average inventory now stands at 60, a 20 percent increase. But at least you will never have a stockout again, right? Wrong. Safety stocks don't get rid of the problem of running short of inventory. Once a company uses safety stock, it becomes a habit which a manufacturer relies upon, instead of attacking the real causes of the shortages in inventory. There are a number of causes, the primary one being wasteful set-up time. Let's look now at what happens to inventory once a set-up program is implemented.

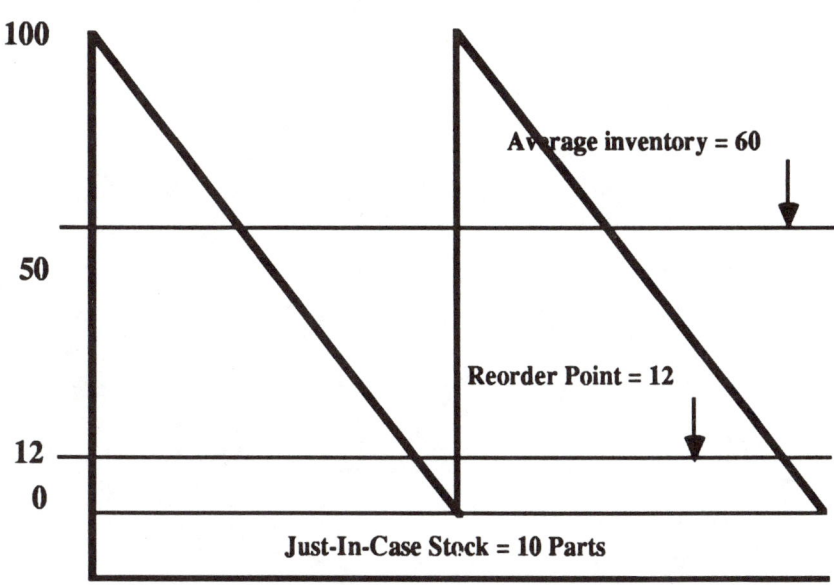

Just-In-Case (JIC) Inventory Management

Let's assume the same criteria as for the previous examples and that it takes 8 hours to perform the changeover. As already stated, the first goal of set-up reduction is to cut the set-up time in half and then to cut the lot size in half. Once achieved, you now make 50 parts instead of 100 as the graph on the next page shows.

Note that, although it takes one half the time to set up, it still takes the same amount of set-up time to make 100 parts because we set up twice during the same period. But, now you only need to stock one half of the inventory that you normally would hold. The average inventory level for this particular example is now at 25 parts, a 50 percent reduction from our first example. Of course, you wouldn't stop here with a set-up program. The next step

Set-Up Reduction

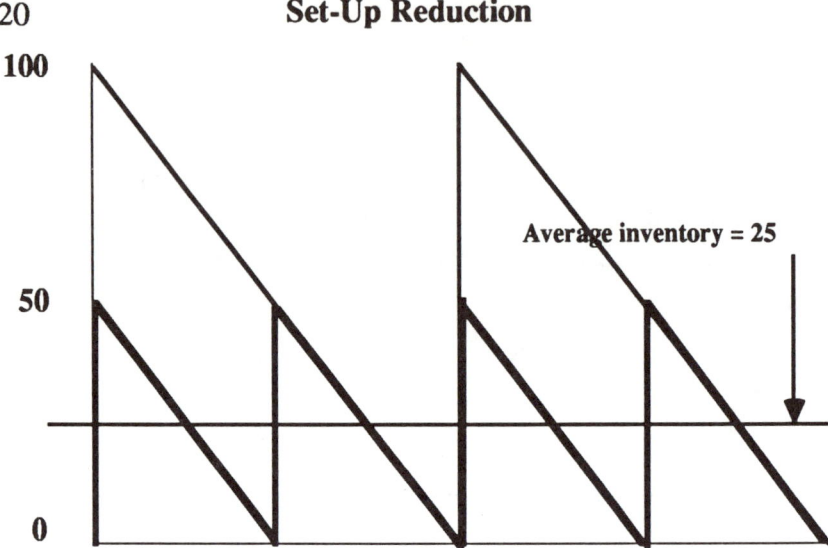

Sawtooth Curve
Set-Up Time And Lot Size Cut In Half

would be to cut the set-up time and lot size in half again as the graph on the next page shows.

Again, it still takes the same time to set up for 100 parts since we do four set-ups, but now the average inventory is 12.5 parts. Now, it is possible for a company like General Foods to manufacture all 15 flavors of their Stovetop Stuffing during one day. General Foods was able to reduce the set-up time on one machine from 4 hours to 10 minutes. The flexibility that this represents means that less inventory is needed because run times don't have to be long to justify the time and cost it would take if the set-up took 4 hours. In addition, the company can produce more volume now if marketing demands it.

Pro-Tech Vice President Mel Pilachowski says that many traditional companies make the mistake of looking at inventory purely

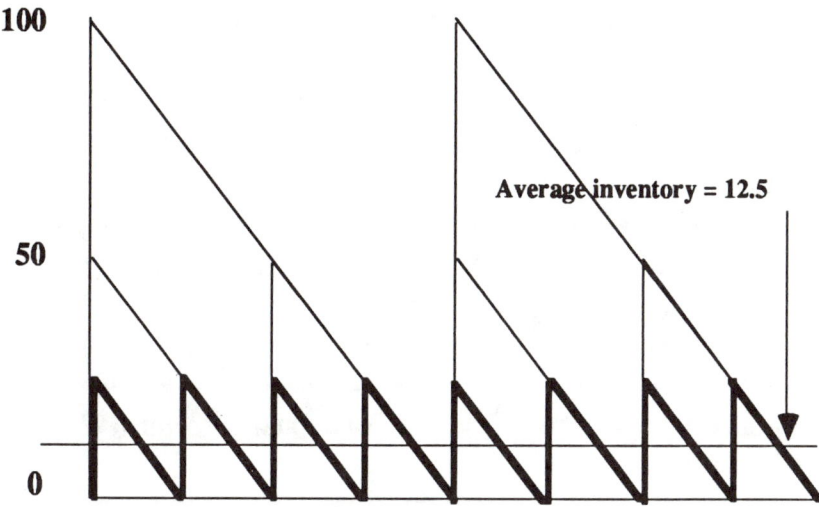

**Sawtooth Curve
Set-Up Time And Lot Size
Cut In Half Again**

as an asset. And it is, but it costs money to carry this asset. Those costs are the inventory carrying costs and the real savings generated by a set-up program are the reduction of these costs. Inventory carrying costs include such items as:

> • **Storage space costs.**
> • **Handling equipment costs for stores.**
> • **Inventory risk costs.**
> • **Inventory service costs.**
> • **Capital costs (cost of borrowing money).**

As noted earlier, carrying costs can account for as much as 30 percent of the total value of the inventory. Set-up reduction will significantly lower that figure by reducing the amount of inventory a company will require.

LEADERSHIP AND COMMITMENT

Without commitment to what we call the Total Business Concept (TBC), set-up reduction is a difficult task. Like any concept that works, TBC is easy to state and comprehend. We define it as:

> **The commitment to eliminate total waste**
> **in the company**
> **by a continuous improvement process.**

TBC also employs the concept of Total Quality Control which is defined as:

> **A total commitment by management**
> **in employing the tools and techniques**
> **of quality throughout the organization,**
> **from top management to the lowest level.**

Both definitions have key phrases which point out the characteristics of leadership in a set-up reduction program. These points can be summed up as the commitment to delegate responsibility and authority to all levels of the organization. Don't be led astray by the belief that management alone is the cause of the problems in your company. After all, who is management? One definition is that management is anybody above me in the organization.

We define management as every person in the company. Look at it this way. A punch press operator manages a punch press, a secretary manages letter-typing, and so on. These people, along with engineers, middle managers and executives, must take the initiative to solve problems. They should be given the resources to identify causes and to correct them.

We are reminded of a situation at one client where a line worker was reluctant to accept our philosophy. "Why?" we asked. "Because nobody listens to our suggestions." We told him to give us a chance and he agreed to. The team of which he was a member was working on a set-up reduction and found that if a new tool was made for them, they could reduce the set-up time dramatically. Now that the company had subscribed to a TBC philosophy, the tool was quickly made for the team.

"What do you think of that?" we asked our reluctant line worker.

"It's great," he said. "They really listened. Just one thing."

"What?" we wanted to know.

"I made this same suggestion ten years ago!"

There's a lesson to be learned from this example. Listen to the operators. It is the best way we know to show both leadership and commitment. Some people will still be reluctant. You will hear responses just like the ones below:

> **Response #1: "But I've always done it that way for the past twenty years."**

> **Response #2: "That set-up would take two hours even for a skilled worker."**

> **Response #3: "You are trying to eliminate my job."**

Response #4: "You are trying to make me look stupid."

Response #5: "You are trying to make me work harder."

To which, we would reply:

Answer #1: "Your competitors are changing. Do you want to be left behind?"

Answer #2: "Ask that skilled operator if he or she can reduce it even more. Invariably, they will say that they can.

Answer #3: "No, we aren't. We're trying to make sure that you have a job in the future and that we have a company to run."

Answer #4: "We guarantee that any documentation of a set-up will be confidential and that it will not be used in any job or merit appraisal."

Answer #5: "No, we are trying to make you more efficient so that both of us can meet the competition."

Simply ask your people to give it a chance and remind them of our favorite business maxim:

> **Those who say "It can be done"**
> **and those who say "It can't be done"**
> **are both guaranteed to be right.**

THE KAWASAKI EXPERIENCE

As part of the management team at Kawasaki in Lincoln, Nebraska, one of us, Jerry Claunch, had first-hand experience of how a set-up reduction program was implemented. What follows is a summary of that experience and an example of what you can do.

The Kawasaki Production Line

The assembly line at Kawasaki looked like an inverted "T." Motorcycle frames began assembly at point A and moved right toward point C. The front fork and front wheel assembly began at

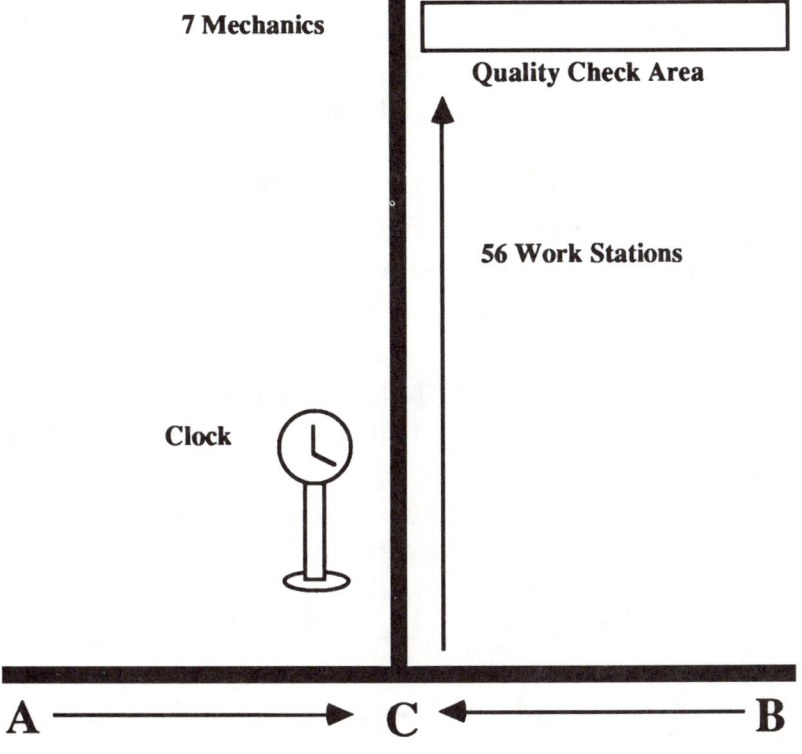

point B and moved left toward C. At point C, the front assembly and frame were put together with front and rear tires attached. This assembly was then placed on a conveyor line which ran through the remaining work stations. At the end of the line, there was another conveyor which ran off to the right. Every motorcycle was placed on this line to be checked by one of a team of seven mechanics. These mechanics would try to start the motorcycle and drive it. If one would not start, the mechanic would push it over to a work area in order to fix the problem.

Employee Involvement Issues

Before we began implementing a set-up reduction program, we had to convince our employees that we meant it when we said that:

NOBODY WILL LOSE HIS OR HER JOB!

Kawasaki told its people that jobs may be eliminated, but that everybody would still be employed. As soon as a job came up because of attrition or increased demand, they would get the job. Before you make this promise at your plant, take time to think about what this really means. It may mean, as it did at Kawasaki, that 36 people were on the payroll with no work to do at the end of the first year. Kawasaki continued to pay these people their wages and their benefits. The company felt that the success of its program rested on the cooperation and trust of its people. How committed or honest would the company have looked if it promised continued employment and then started to balk when the numbers rose? The company also knew, however, that it was saving money on the production side because it was producing quality motorcycles with less waste. Nevertheless, Kawasaki would have looked bad in its people's eyes, if it reneged on its promise. How much effort would a team put into solving a problem if they thought they were working themselves out of a job?

Implementation Steps

1. Kawasaki told the mechanics that it wanted to eliminate their jobs by helping to produce zero-defect motorcycles. The company assured them that they would still be employed and that Kawasaki had to take measures to meet the competition.

2. The company slowed down the line and put up a clock with a 3-foot diameter which only ran when the line wasn't running.

3. The company told the mechanics that when they found a defect, it was their job to talk to the person or persons responsible. In other words, the mechanics' job was to start a problem-solving process.

4. In order to solve the problem, sometimes the line had to stop. Kawasaki had already installed 56 stop buttons on the line, one at each work station. It took two months to convince people that it was OK to stop the line whenever they encountered a problem or weren't sure about quality.

5. Wherever the line was stopped, three people from either side came over as well as the supervisor to help solve the problem. The supervisor's job was to document why the line stopped and then to decide whether the gathered team had the resources to solve the problem then and there. If it could, the goal was that the line would never stop again for the same reason. If it could not be solved by

this team, the supervisor pulled a team together with the skills and abilities to solve the problem. This team consisted of management and direct labor.

Set-Up Reduction

Many of the problems which the teams worked on were set-up problems. Kawasaki had a 4-hour changeover on its production line to switch from one model of motorcycle to another model. To give you an idea of how the company worked to reduce the set-up time, let's assume that it is Monday morning and the plant has just begun to manufacture 1,000 cc models. Prior to set-up reduction, whenever we set up for one particular model, we would run an EOQ (Economic Order Quantity) batch of 1,000 units. Let's say that about 11:30 a.m., we get a call from Marketing.

"We need to fill orders from our dealers for 650 cc models. Start building them."

"No problem," we would tell Marketing. "We will finish making the 1,000s early Wednesday afternoon. Then we will do the changeover and start making 650s on Thursday morning."

"You don't understand our business," Marketing would say. "Our dealers don't only carry Kawasaki motorcycles. They have Hondas, Suzukis, and Yamahas, too. If they are out of Kawasaki 650s, they will sell a 650 cc motorcycle but it will be one of our competitor's. We will lose a sale and possibly a customer forever."

"You don't understand manufacturing," we would say. "We have 4-hour changeovers. We have to run 1,000 units to justify the cost and the time. You're asking me at 11:30 a.m. on Monday to tear down the line and start making another model? It won't work. Give us a more accurate forecast for a longer period of time."

Of course, if anybody was able to forecast accurately over a long period of time, they would never have to work again. They would be billionaires. So what were we to do? We jointly decided to work on producing a 20-day schedule. That was possible when we had reduced our set-up time so that we could make all the models every day. This is exactly what the Brothers manufacturing plant does in Japan as Peter L. Grieco, Jr., and Michael W. Gozzo, ProTech founders, discovered on one of their fact-finding tours of the Far East. At this plant, there is a production line where you can see typewriters, printers and sewing machines all on the same line. Brothers can do this because it has reduced the set-up to such a small interval of time that it is no problem to switch over a machine from working on a typewriter to working on a sewing machine. That degree of flexibility is our goal and set-up reduction enables us to attain it.

Set-up reduction enables us to improve quality and keep up with our competition. The future will belong to those companies which are flexible. The funding for this change will come from the reduced costs of carrying lower levels of inventory which are a result of set-up reduction. It can do the same and more for your company. Let's look next at a working definition of set-up reduction.

CHAPTER TWO

ESTABLISHING THE FOUNDATION FOR SET-UP REDUCTION

Isaac Newton once proclaimed that he could only see as far as he could because he stood on the shoulders of those who came before him. The same philosophy is true of set-up reduction. Set-up time is relatively easy to define:

> **The time from the last good part of the previous run until the first good part of the next run is made at a normal efficiency rate.**

This definition may sound simple, but let's take a look at what it really means. When a component is being manufactured and the final piece from the previous run is produced, we can then start to measure the time elapsed until we get the first good part from the next new job. All the time in between the last good piece and first good piece of the new set-up must be measured.

Set-up reduction, then, must incorporate all of the following actions into one integrated unit in order to achieve the desired results:

> • **Simple job changes.**
>
> • **Focus on equipment up-time.**
>
> • **Lot-for-lot production.**
>
> • **Increased flexibility.**
>
> • **No reduction of people.**
>
> • **Teamwork approach.**
>
> • **Operators and/or set-up people are focal point.**
>
> • **Videotape the process.**

These activities, however, cannot be fully understood without building a foundation to support them. The "shoulders" which set-up reduction rests upon can be divided into three main classifications—Customer Satisfaction, Lead Time and Total Cost Management. It should be noted here that although the terms *set-up*, *changeover* and *make-ready* are used by different industries, they are interchangeable in this book. The basic principles behind all three are identical and meet the same definition given above.

THE FOUNDATION OF SET-UP REDUCTION

Just as you wouldn't perform a set-up without the correct tools, so you shouldn't implement a set-up reduction program without the proper tools. Let's review the building blocks (which are in no particular order) in the foundation of a set-up reduction program.

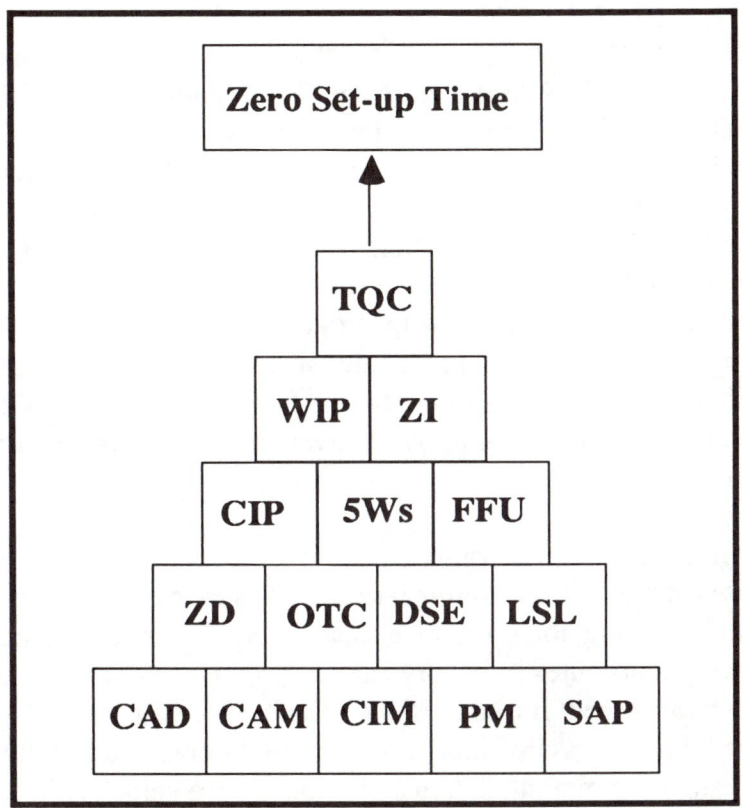

TOTAL QUALITY CONTROL (TQC)

TQC is not the inspection of parts to see whether they conform to requirements. It is better defined as the analysis of the processes and operations of a company in the manufacturing of components or material. Quality begins with designing tooling and defining the production process and goes through the process of set-up. We must address set-up scrap pieces and eliminate that waste.

WORK-IN-PROCESS (WIP)

There are different types of inventory in a plant: **Purchased Material** and **Raw Material** (from outside suppliers), **Finished Goods**, and **WIP Inventory**. Inventory is waste. It should be reduced through a program of lot size reduction. Set-up reduction moves manufacturers toward a lot size of one. Ideally, once material arrives at a work station, equipment can be changed over quickly so that the material never has time to be in queue. The secret is to establish a set-up program early in the JIT/TQC process. Don't get caught reducing lot size without reducing set-up time as well. This also holds true for your suppliers. With a strong program in place, WIP inventory will soon virtually disappear.

By eliminating the economic impact of set-up or lot sizing, we can revise the practice of running large lot sizes for overhead absorption. Producing lot sizes in excess of customer requirements actually contributes inventory carrying costs to overhead which must be absorbed! If it sounds like a Catch 22 to you, you're right. In addition, excess inventory must be warehoused and warehousing is nothing more than transportation at zero velocity.

ZERO INVENTORY (ZI)

Zero inventory means setting a level of inventory which is still able to meet customer demand. In many cases, zero is not zero, but the attainment of an acceptable level of inventory. Companies should continuously strive to improve themselves in their quest for this goal. We must make progress to get the inventory to the lowest level without disappointing customers or employees. We do not accomplish this overnight.

All too often, companies spend their valuable resources attempting to control inventory, rather than attempting to eliminate the causes for its existence. We should understand that most inventory exists because we don't know what we are doing. We don't know when purchased materials will be delivered, whether all parts will meet specifications, whether machinery will be operational, etc. In order to focus properly upon the value-added nature of inventory, we should rename the inventory control department and call it the "I don't know what I'm doing" department.

CONTINUOUS IMPROVEMENT PROCESS (CIP)

CIP is the process whereby companies strive for improvement, never being satisfied until they have improved the process. CIP is a key acronym in a set-up reduction program. It is almost synonymous with commitment. We often hear companies say that they are going to get a set-up program running in one year as though that is a long time. It is not a long time from a CIP perspective. For one thing, the statement implies that the program will be over one year after its starting date. Nothing is further from the truth. For committed companies, it will take many years to reach the goal of zero set-up time.

This doesn't mean that you won't get improvements in less than one year. It means that you aren't finished after those first few reductions. When we run up against this attitude that a company doesn't have to keep striving for improvement, we remind them of Toyota. Toyota started its JIT program in 1949. Are they finished yet? Absolutely not! At Kawasaki in Nebraska, they reduced the set-up time on a punch press from 45 minutes to 45 seconds. The last time we checked back, they were still looking at ways to improve. That's commitment to CIP. Of course, the closer we get to zero, the harder the improvements come.

At some point, a company will need to make an investment in order to keep the reduction of set-up time moving forward. But, in the beginning, the only investment needed is an investment in people. Specifically, this investment means allowing people to review each set-up, to evaluate it and to come up with ideas about how to reduce the time it takes to change over.

Computer enthusiasts, by the way, will understand one of our favorite analogies. CIP is a "positive DO loop" from which a company never wishes to exit.

WHY? WHY? WHY? WHY? WHY? (5Ws)—Our goal is to find the low cost/no cost solution to reduce set-up times. People who participate on a team must be able to ask "Why?" many, many times to determine the cause of a problem. And whatever the response is to the first "Why?", they should then automatically ask "Why?" again. An organization must be open to communication that challenges the status quo. People should feel free to ask: Why do we do it that way? Why do we use these tools? Why don't we repair that equipment? Why? Why? Why?

Training in identification of improvement areas is vital to the discovery of low cost/no cost solutions. Our experience has shown, however, that companies which train and then encourage their people to ask "Why?" are the companies with the highest degree of success. If you think back to your days as a two-year-old, you can easily understand the 5 Why technique. It is the way we learn.

FITNESS FOR USE (FFU)

FFU says that equipment, materials and parts should be appropriate for the use for which they were intended. In other words, they should not be forced to work for you in ways in which they were not originally intended. Having the correct tooling available is of paramount importance in the set-up process. Companies often use a great deal of material or tools which is not fit for use. Sometimes this is because they assume that commonly used tools will always be where they should be and in good repair. Too many companies, however, don't always maintain tools in the ready-for-use category.

During a recent fact-finding trip to Japan, we witnessed several companies that have totally eliminated set-ups from their process. All equipment, tooling and fixtures were maintained in perfect working order. You will never be able to do set-ups more quickly if you don't have the proper tools. There are three questions to ask in this area:

> - **Are the tools, equipment, material, etc. available for use?**
> - **Is it the right tool, fixture, clamping method, etc. for the job?**
> - **Is it fit for use from a maintenance perspective? Don't assume a tool is properly maintained simply because it's available in the right place.**

ZERO DEFECTS (ZD)

ZD, in essence, is virtually the same as TQC and is the result of a quality set-up. When Jerry worked as a machine operator, he was told that the production rate standard for his machine was 96 parts per hour. After work each day during his training period, he would exit under a sign that read: *Quality—Would You Buy What You*

Built Today? At first, Jerry would say to himself, "I'm only going to build quality parts that I would want to buy." When Jerry is out on the line, however, his machine is always breaking down, tooling must be fixed or it takes hours to do a change-over. Consequently, he's never quite up to 96 parts. His supervisor comes over and tells him he's got to pick up the pace. Now, when Jerry leaves the plant, he doesn't see the sign any more. It's still there, but all Jerry can think about is getting up to 96 parts. When the supervisor is only concerned with quantity, then the employee is only concerned with quantity.

The solution is to allow time for the employee to produce quality parts and to work on the process to reduce set-up time. A quick change mentality should be encouraged, instead of a production at any cost mentality.

ONE TOUCH CHANGEOVER (OTC)

The aim of OTC is to make easy adjustments on a piece of equipment when it changes over from one product to another. No more setting the tool, trying a part, resetting, retrying and so on. You should be able to put the tool in place with one touch, clamp it and start making parts. The point, of course, is to make it right the first time.

An example of OTC is switching from 2-wheel to 4-wheel drive. In a Ford Bronco, there is an option for the driver to push a button or switch. Earlier 4-wheel drive changeovers required getting out of the vehicle and manually turning the front wheel hubs. The Japanese, by the way, add this option at no cost. Why do we in America have to pay extra?

Most machinery purchases are focused upon infinite adjustability as a positive attribute for flexibility. We buy infinitely adjustable equipment and then run a limited variety of parts. OTC focuses on simplification and minimization of adjustments.

DIFFERENT SET OF EYES (DSE)

In order to make a set-up reduction program work in a facility, a company is going to want employees who are generalists. They should understand a lot of things in a lot of areas and how to do a number of tasks. This makes them into an ideal DSE to put on your set-up team. They are fresh and they have innovative ideas. They naturally employ the 5Ws approach defined above. In fact, don't hesitate to use employees who don't work on the shop floor. They are often an ideal DSE because they have no preconceived notions and ask "why?" many more than five times.

An ideal team to work on quick changeovers would consist of generalists, but most of our companies have no real generalists. Therefore, we must put specialists together to form a "generalist" team. When we ask people to be on a team, we need to show respect for their knowledge. At one company, we came into contact with a set-up person with over 25 years of experience. We told him about all the improvements he could accomplish with a set-up reduction program and then asked him if he had any ideas. He told us in no uncertain terms about what we could do with our program. He didn't want any management person telling him how to do his job. Eventually, we were able to convince him that we weren't telling him how to do his job and that we only wanted to help him make it easier. That's why we needed his input. We would have been foolish not to tap the wealth of knowledge that this man had, knowledge which eventually greatly aided the set-up program at that company.

LEADER SPEAKS LAST (LSL)

In order for DSE to work in a team environment, a company also needs to observe the rules of participation that the leader speaks last. When top management is placed on a team, they normally do all the talking and directing. We tell our clients not to allow that to happen on a team. We want top management to do two things when they find themselves on a set-up reduction team—listen and talk, but do a lot more listening than talking and don't talk until everybody else has had their chance. At one client, Peter L. Grieco Jr, the president and CEO of Pro-Tech (Professionals for Technology Associates, Inc.), leaned over and whispered into the president's ear. "You're talking too much and giving only your answer to the issue," Pete told the surprised executive. We aren't recommending that you tell your top management to be totally quiet, nor are we advocating that you allow an hourly worker to get up on his or her soapbox and monopolize a team meeting. We do advocate that management participate, but let those closest to the process help fix the problem. All you need to do is explain one rule up front—**Equal Participation!**

COMPUTER AIDED DESIGN (CAD)
COMPUTER AIDED MANUFACTURING (CAM)
COMPUTER INTEGRATED MANUFACTURING (CIM)

CAD uses the computer to help in the design of parts and components. CAM aids in setting up the manufacturing process for CNC (Computer Numerically Controlled) equipment. CIM is the integration of robotics, computers and automation. The rule for CAD, CAM and CIM is to be judicious in their application. That is, if you need a computer, get it and use it. If you don't need a computer, don't get one. Don't buy computers or computer software packages because it's the latest thing. Don't get MRP (Material Requirements Planning) or MRP II (Manufacturing Resource Planning) because it's the latest buzzword. Don't buy robots because someone else is buying them. Don't even do cellular technology just because everybody else is. Get the point? Then remember this rule:

DO "IT"
(CAD, CAM, CIM, ROBOTICS, ETC.)
ONLY BECAUSE YOU NEED "IT"
FOR YOUR BUSINESS.

SUPPLIERS AS PARTNERS (SAP)

One of the most frequent questions we are asked when we present the JIT foundation of set-up reduction is whether JIT really means that your inventory won't increase because you have forced your suppliers to increase theirs. Our answer is this:

IF YOUR SUPPLIERS' INVENTORY INCREASES
AS A RESULT OF YOUR PROGRAM,
THEN YOUR PROGRAM ISN'T WORKING.

We advocate that both you and your suppliers enter into a win/win, set-up reduction partnership with each other. Stress that their production schedule should be in sync with your own. Give them long-term contracts and share product and process information, but demand that you receive material of 100 percent quality delivered to the right place in the right quantities at the right time.

Supplier involvement cannot be stressed enough. After all, 50 to 80 percent of most companies' material content comes form outside the plant. How can we expect to achieve major benefits if we ignore external suppliers? Obviously, a supplier cannot do this alone. What you really want in a SAP program is for your suppliers to do what you are doing. Help them by starting to work with them on set-up reduction and quality soon after you have made your initial attempts. Then they can benefit from your experience. Hold a Supplier's Day in which you educate them and explain what you are doing, what set-up reduction is really all about, and what the goals and objectives are.

In the book, **Supplier Certification:** *Achieving Excellence* (PT Publications, Palm Beach Gardens, FL), the authors show how to form such a partnership with your suppliers. In the book, it also becomes clear that CIP and JIT together make what could be called the Golden Rule of business: *It's good business for you if your supplier's business does better.* After all, you don't want your suppliers to build up inventory levels and pass on the costs of carrying all that inventory to you in the form of higher prices.

PREVENTIVE MAINTENANCE (PM)

The crux of PM is the analysis of mean time between failures. Companies should be gathering data for these reports and if they aren't, they should begin immediately. It can be computerized, but it isn't necessary. Manually collected records are just as effective. The key is to gather data and to review this data at regular intervals to determine the time between failures. From the review, companies will be able to make decisions. They can determine the life of a belt, a bearing or a gear by looking at the frequency of replacement in the past. Then, they can start replacing equipment parts during down time or during scheduled maintenance time. In other words, fix the equipment just before it is expected to break. We call this zero breakdown maintenance.

General Foods Before Set-Up Reduction

Once the failure rate is determined, you should start working with your production schedule people to get the necessary time to repair a machine in order to perform preventive maintenance. Also, bear in mind that often when you observe a set-up, it contains maintenance issues. If it is a maintenance issue, don't make it a set-up issue by working around it or rigging up something that hides the problem. Don't kid yourself. The problem is still there and it possibly will get worse. It should be emphasized that if maintenance schedule attainment is not measured and enforced with the same degree of discipline as production, then "zero-breakdown" maintenance will not work.

LEAD TIME, LOT SIZES AND SET-UP REDUCTION

Set-up reduction is inextricably linked to lead time and lot sizes. The intent of set-up reduction is to reduce production set-up times in order to support a movement toward small lot sizes, less lead time and improved productivity. The following principles are at work in the interaction of these three areas:

1. Smaller lot sizes necessitate faster changeovers of equipment.
2. Smaller lot sizes require more set-ups which places an emphasis on JIT delivery to the operation.
3. Sound procurement decisions must be based on real need and quality rather than price.
4. Long set-ups require long runs which translates

into higher inventory and associated carrying costs.

5. Reduced set-ups result in shorter runs which translates into less inventory.

Set-up reduction can be best accomplished by developing a team of people, supported by management, which, among other tasks, works to insure the delivery of quality parts in the right quantity at the right time at the right total cost. That means frequent, small deliveries directly to the production line in order to reduce inventories. To do so, however, is of no value until the factory floor is able to wean itself from long production runs in favor of flexible manufacturing. In flexible manufacturing, machine operators must be able to reduce set-up time so that production can quickly change from producing one item to another to dovetail with customer requirements. Therefore:

> **The ideal manufacturing objective is to perform set-ups so quickly that lot sizes of one can be accomplished.**

To obtain levels approaching that ideal requires a persistent attack on lead time since shorter lead times mean that inventory turns over faster, resulting in a greater return on assets.

Lead time, itself, breaks down into 5 components:

Queue — time material is staged ahead of a work center waiting for its turn to be set up and run.

Set-up — process of getting the machine ready to run the part — the time from the last good part to the first good part at normal efficiency rate.

Run — time actually spent processing parts at a work center and adding value.

Wait — time the parts sit after processing and before being moved to the next work center. This is a function of lot size. If there is a lot size of 50, the first processed part must wait until the other 49 are finished before it can be moved.

Move — time spent moving parts to the next work center where the parts enter a queue again.

Out of these five components, real work is actually done only during run time as the graph below shows.

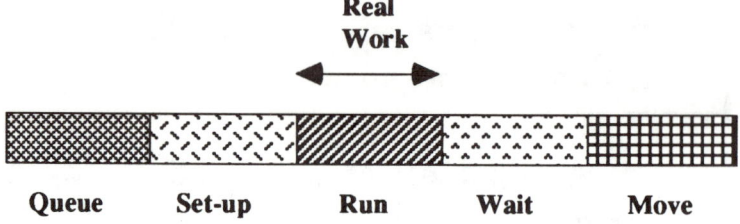

By reducing set-up time, we also reduce lot sizes which means that we can shrink the space representing wait time by a corresponding percentage.

Likewise, we can shrink move time as well since we now move smaller quantities more frequently. In other words, there is less WIP inventory.

The idea of reducing queue time is difficult for employees to accept because we keep running out of the right material today even though we have high queues. Queue time can be reduced to some degree, however, simply because there is less material in the queue. Significant reductions can be obtained if a company is able to get parts to a work station during set-up.

Here, then, is what we have accomplished—lead time before set-up reduction and after set-up reduction:

LEAD TIME (BEFORE)

Queue	Set-up	Run	Wait	Move

LEAD TIME (AFTER)

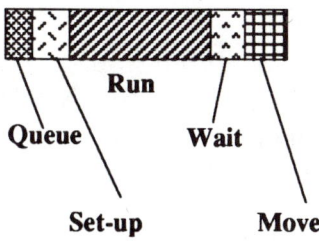

As you can see, we haven't even begun to address run time and yet we have significantly reduced lead time without talking about bigger, faster and better (and more expensive!) pieces of equipment. You shouldn't buy improvement. After all, a company could eliminate set-up time altogether simply by buying dedicated equipment. All it costs is money. If you have a few hundred million dollars to spare, go ahead.

We're suggesting that you can get the same results by using the brainpower stored in the minds of your people. One day at a client, for example, a set-up team was meeting in the production area.

They were discussing the purchase of some conveyors to make it easier to get parts from one work station to another. A woman who had worked on the line overheard us.

"Did you ever think," she said, "of moving the equipment closer together so we could hand the parts to each other?"

That's a brainstorm. A simple idea that all the experts had missed. That was also an excellent example of the concept of DSE, or Different Set of Eyes.

LEAD TIME OBJECTIVES

Lead time represents a costly utilization of a wide variety of company resources. Its reduction is both a vital quality control and cost reduction opportunity and an opportunity to truly meet customer demand. The following are the objectives of a lead time reduction process:

REDUCE OR ELIMINATE SET-UP.

> Set-up is a non-productive, income-using element of lead time. It impedes the response by a company to customer requirements and negatively impacts line and machine efficiency. Furthermore, it increases "buffer" inventory requirements. On a positive note, set-up reduction allows you to unleash all those hidden benefits of producing at lower cost and shorter time.

IMPROVE MATERIAL HANDLING.

> Material handling is a non-productive use of resources.

It should be minimized using the same principles as employed in set-up reduction. The goal is reduce the quantity of material moved and thus simplify material handling.

MATCH LOT SIZES TO CUSTOMER DEMAND.

Reductions in lead time allow you to approach the smallest lot size of one part. In essence, the goal is to produce exactly what the customer orders. No more, no less!

REDUCE WORK-IN-PROCESS (WIP).

Reduction of WIP inventories through accelerated production flow reduces inventory carrying costs, demands control of quality and reduces the amount of space needed for manufacturing.

REDUCE ALL INVENTORIES.

An across-the-board reduction in inventory allows a company to use its limited resources in more productive ways. Those resources include labor, machines, materials and capital.

TOTAL COST MANAGEMENT

What is the value of having the reputation of being a producer of quality products which are delivered quickly and on time in the required quantity? How much does excess inventory cost? Questions like these are actually variants of one central question:

```
┌─────────────────────────────────────────┐
│ ┌─────────────────────────────────────┐ │
│ │      HOW DO I REDUCE WASTE          │ │
│ │   AND SATISFY MY CUSTOMERS?         │ │
│ └─────────────────────────────────────┘ │
└─────────────────────────────────────────┘
```

HOW DO I REDUCE WASTE AND SATISFY MY CUSTOMERS?

Total cost management is built on the premise of reducing waste and of becoming more efficient and accurate.

Current cost management has served all types of organizations. It has survived because of its ability to capture, record, measure and communicate the cost of operating a business. Cost management has remained the same through the years as the business environment has changed. This has led to the need for new ideas and concepts to help us measure and predict our operations. And, to cost justify improvements in new methods and implementations.

We define cost management as:

>   1. **The management of cost whether or not the cost has direct impact on inventory or the financial statement.**

>   2. **Management's commitment to the continual reduction of the elements of cost whether or not those costs can be measured in purely financial terms.**

TOTAL COST

In keeping with this definition of cost management, the definition of cost has changed as well. Cost is now defined as total cost, or *all cost attributable to the sale, manufacturing and distribution of products*, as the diagram on the next page demonstrates.

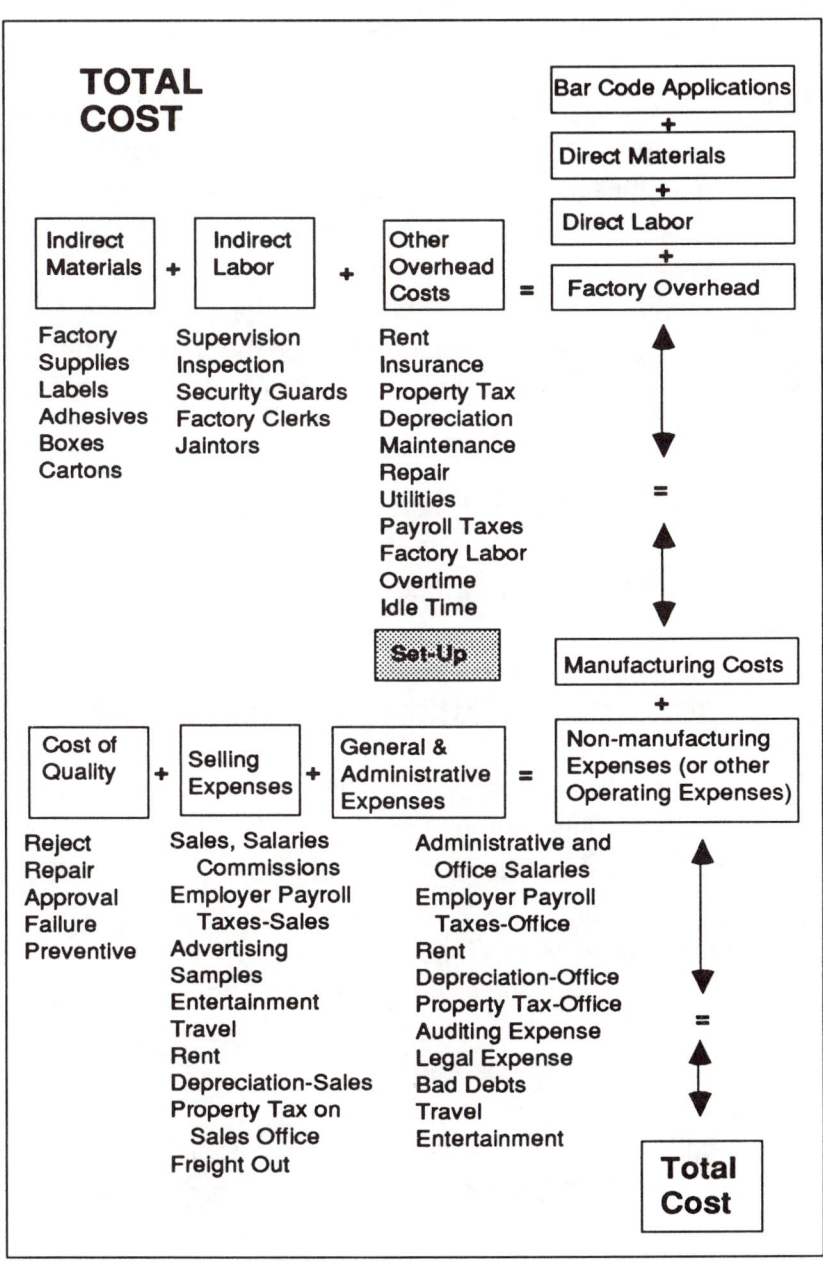

This definition moves companies away from a dependence on price analysis as the major criterion for determining costs. This is because cost analysis examines all costs involved in the process of manufacturing products, whereas price analysis uses the selling price without examining or evaluating the separate elements of cost and profit which make up the price. In the past, accountants looked for ways to absorb set-up cost. You must recognize that the EOQ formula drives up inventory levels predicated on set-up dollars. Now with set-up being performed more frequently, why worry about how many set-ups are done per day as long as we work eight hours a day.

SET-UP REDUCTION COST IMPROVEMENT

Financial control becomes a much simpler task as we focus on cost improvement:

9-STEP COST IMPROVEMENT METHOD

1. Identify Targets and Opportunities for Set-up Reduction.
2. Describe Them in Detail.
3. Identify and Define Possible Problems—People, Tools, Equipment.
4. Set Objectives and Goals.
5. Gather Facts and other Related Information and Analyze the Data.
6. Determine Solutions.
7. Evaluate Solutions and Alternatives.
8. Implement Techniques to Reduce Set-up.
9. Evaluate and Measure Results all the Time (Ongoing Program).

Cost management begins by identifying set-up targets. Second, the team will describe the targets. The aim here is to note all costs, apparent and hidden, which are associated with the target. Third, define the problems you are experiencing within these areas so that, fourth, you can set objectives. As with set-up reduction, the rule of halves applies here as well. That is, you should seek to reach your goal by reaching a point half way between where you start and where you want to be. Once achieved, the new point becomes half the remaining distance to the goal. In other words, the first objective is to reduce set-up time by 50 percent, and then 50 percent again.

Fifth, gather facts which will enable you to suggest possible solutions and analyze the data. Coming up with these hypotheses is the sixth step. Seventh, evaluate your solutions. This is where the team becomes vitally important. Any solution you choose will have effects throughout the company. Have people on hand who can tell you how it will affect the operations and procedures in their individual departments. Of course, some areas are more greatly affected than others. Therefore, it is not necessary to have the whole company sit down and debate the merits and demerits of a proposed solution. Each company will find an optimum size for the team and a most effective make-up. Our recommendation is five to nine people.

Eighth, implement the set-up solution which the team has determined to be the most effective at cutting costs. Needless to say, the implementation, itself, must be cost-effective as well. Ninth and last, evaluate the results of your implementation and move on to the next target set-up.

HOW TO IDENTIFY TARGETS

The improvement framework will help you identify a number of targets requiring attention. Although we find that many companies (whether large or small, whether food processors or manufacturers of office furniture) have similar problems, we also realize that the dynamics of your particular situation will have a great impact on your solutions. That is why it so important to use a team to understand the dynamics of set-up reduction.

TARGETS	Number of Transactions	Cost per Transaction	Savings
Absenteeism			
Turnover			
Accidents			
Distribution			
Warehousing			
Mail			
Maintenance			
Materials			
Supplies			
Meetings			
Paperwork			
Purchasing			
Quality			
Telephones			
Time management			

Improvements must be long-term. The chart on the preceding page indicates some typical targets which support set-up reduction in all areas of the company. Keep in mind that set-up can be achieved in areas other than manufacturing. Office applications, for example, are a fruitful area.

Other areas which can be added as targets are energy, equipment, and facilities. The Far East, which is not blessed as we are with abundant resources, has been pressured to make dramatic improvements here. Part of the team's job will be to forecast where constraints will occur which may have deleterious effects on the company.

Many of the areas in the list above are more people-related, that is, those items which people use to help them do their job. In this list, we have telephone service, office supplies, time management, meetings, and paperwork. Although you may say that each of these areas has a small effect, their sum can be considerable. Ignoring set-up reduction in areas other than manufacturing would be like telling a race car driver to ignore a few protruding screws or door handles on his automobile. One screw may not cause much drag, but a lot of them combined with other small, protruding shapes will greatly increase air resistance. That means the car will not run as efficiently or as fast. The smart racer will pay attention to details in order to win the race.

Improvement is a many-lapped race, perhaps like the Indianapolis 500, but more like a sports car rally. In a rally, drivers must arrive at designated checkpoints at certain times. Winners are those racers who most closely follow the rally's instructions. Not only does this mean pinpoint timing, but accurate routing. The same can apply to a company on the course of cost improvement. Your navigator, or financial analyst, can help you stay on route so that you will arrive on time at checkpoints.

PERFORMANCE MEASUREMENTS

How do we know if we are winning the war against waste? By measuring our performance. We must measure performance to be predictable, so that we know what we have done, where we are and where we are going. It is possible, of course, to measure the wrong areas as is pointed out in *Relevance Lost*, by Johnson and Kaplan. Vice President Mel Pilachowski of Professionals for Technology Associates says that the problem with the old yardsticks of performance measurements is that they are not looking at total cost solutions when talking about set-up reduction. They look only at productivity levels and use a reactive, rather than a proactive approach.

Today, we must develop new yardsticks which provide information to make decisions. Then, we will be able to compare actual results against predicted results and performance. This is best accomplished through a system of measurement that reflects a Total Business Concept. In general, the use of TBC measurements will show:

1. How close we are to reducing set-up to zero. How both internal and external Manufacturing operations have performed. Current information coupled with supplier involvement will provide a new approach.

2. How accurate our reporting and measuring of data are.

We all know that a small mistake compounds over time. Unlike interest on your personal investments, this is not favorable. The surveyor who makes a mistake of one degree can cost you many valuable acres of land.

3. How much set-up waste remains in Manufacturing operations. Waste (set-up), today, is too often accepted as a given and absorbed into product and overhead costs. This is truly a reactive way of thinking and must change in order to compete in a world market.

4. How actual production performance compares to the stated plan. Observing this variance is instrumental in making new plans which require problem solving. Those who don't learn from the mistakes of the past are doomed to repeat them.

These new yardsticks are based on total cost. In essence, Mel Pilachowski points out, this is the same as measuring the performance of the whole company. Our principal thrust is to emphasize a total cost approach, rather than a price-oriented approach.

There are two principles behind cost improvement. One, we should not look at set-up cost alone in seeking to maximize profits, but include the cost of quality, inventory and logistics. Two, we should measure variances against total cost, as well as set-up cost when evaluating our profitability. These two principles work in tandem with the basic principles of JIT/TQC, that is, build to demand and eliminate excess inventory and wasteful operations.

In a nutshell, total cost accounting reduces overhead to less than five percent and categorizes all former components of overhead into specific costs. It will serve a company well in supporting its set-up reduction program to organize accounting into a total cost system.

CHAPTER THREE

GETTING STARTED

Manufacturing companies have traditionally been broken down into three categories—Repetitive, Discrete/Job Shop, and Process/Continuous Flow. Set-up reduction is equally valid in all three types of companies. Whatever the type of manufacturer, both the implementation and maintenance of a set-up reduction program requires a company where continuous improvement is the business philosophy. In such companies, set-up reduction replaces the traditional ways of doing business with a new manufacturing philosophy, but let's first define how set-up effects the three categories of manufacturers.

REPETITIVE MANUFACTURING

A *repetitive* manufacturer is a company in which the production of discrete units are planned and executed via a production schedule, usually at relatively high speeds and volumes. Material tends to flow in a sequential flow. A significant number of the manufacturers in this country are repetitive. In many of them, set-up is constant because machines are always running and producing at high volumes.

This does not mean that there isn't room for improvement or that set-up reduction is not highly important to repetitive manufacturers. At Apple Computer, for example, set-up reduction was defined as Zero Set-Up or changeovers done in minutes and seconds. And Apple made it work. Without any required changeovers or set-up time, Apple was able to create a production line where a 110-volt domestic model was followed by a 220-volt model for Europe.

DISCRETE/JOB SHOP MANUFACTURING

A *discrete/job shop* manufacturer is a functional organization in which departments or work centers are organized around particular types of equipment or operations, such as drilling, forging, spinning or assembling. Products flow through departments in batches corresponding to individual orders which can be either stock orders or customer orders. Typically, 60 to 70 percent of the batches are stock orders with the remaining 30 to 40 percent relegated to discrete customer orders. Set-up time reduction and

quick changeovers are also important to these industries. In order
to survive, job shops have had to move toward a Just-In-Time
environment in which smaller lot sizes must be run. As we have
already seen, smaller lot sizes are best achieved through a program
which reduces set-up time.

PROCESS/CONTINUOUS FLOW MANUFACTURING

A *process/continuous flow* manufacturer has a production system in which the production equipment is organized and se-
quenced according to the steps involved in producing the product.
The term denotes that material flow is continuous during the
production process, that routings of jobs are fixed and that set-ups
are seldom changed. However, set-up times in process industries
are often measured in terms of days. A set-up reduction program
can help bring the amount of time needed to change over equipment down to hours and, at times, even minutes.

Some process manufacturers, such as the cosmetics and food
industries, however, are required to perform many set-ups. These
set-ups are not done for financial or manufacturing reasons, but
because these industries are required by the Environmental Pro-
tection Agency, the Food and Drug Administration and other
federal agencies to follow regulations which require extensive
cleaning as part of the process. The lesson here is that just because
you are a process manufacturer, that does not mean that set-up
reduction can't help you. On the contrary, it is just as vital in the
food and cosmetics industries as it is in metal fabrication or
electronics production.

FLEXIBLE MANUFACTURING

The new philosophy mentioned above, which incorporates quick change and which will replace the traditional categories, is called *flexible manufacturing*. Flexible manufacturers are capable of responding or conforming to change in demand or changes in the manufacturing environment which allow quick turnaround and little, if any set-up time. This is the objective manufacturers should strive for. Flexible manufacturing gets us away from relying upon the accuracy of long-range forecasting by Marketing. Set-up reduction in this environment lowers lot sizes which allows companies to shorten the forecast horizon and meet changes in customer demand much more quickly. In the flexible environment, changeovers are done so quickly that the production line is able to produce precisely what has been ordered by the customers each and every time with no more build to stock.

HOW TO BECOME FLEXIBLE

There are five major strategies to pursue in order to become a flexible manufacturer. Many companies do not view organization and people issues as important. We have found that in preparing a company to move toward flexible manufacturing that it is necessary to install an aggressive program which eliminates set-up in the factory design stage. This will allow a company to respond quickly to changes in customer demand. The path which we have found to be the most successful one at many plants includes the following five major strategies:

<u>ORGANIZING FOR RESULTS</u>

- **Educate all people about the project to form a strong foundation and establish objectives.**
- **Create enthusiasm for the project by delegating authority and responsibility.**
- **Provide a proven method that can be easily implemented.**
- **Establish measurements that show the success of a program and the opportunities for further improvement.**
- **Press for results—challenge people.**

SUPPLIER SET-UP PROGRAMS

Companies must involve suppliers as partners in their set-up reduction programs. It is important to remember, however, that most suppliers have not spent time reducing lead time and lot sizes through a set-up reduction program of their own. Companies with an existing program will have to show their suppliers that the future success of their individual programs depends upon the development of supplier and customer partnerships. Suppliers must make quick change a reality in their own plants. There is no better learning experience than the example of success.

Set-up reduction is both an *internal* and *external* program. A successful set-up reduction program demands that the internal flow of material be as orderly as the flow from external suppliers. What is true for the supplier side will also be true for the customer to whom you supply finished items. You will be required to respond quickly to their needs (on-time delivery of 100 percent quality products in the quantity needed).

The following diagram shows the critical set-up issues which occur as material moves in the supplier/customer relationship:

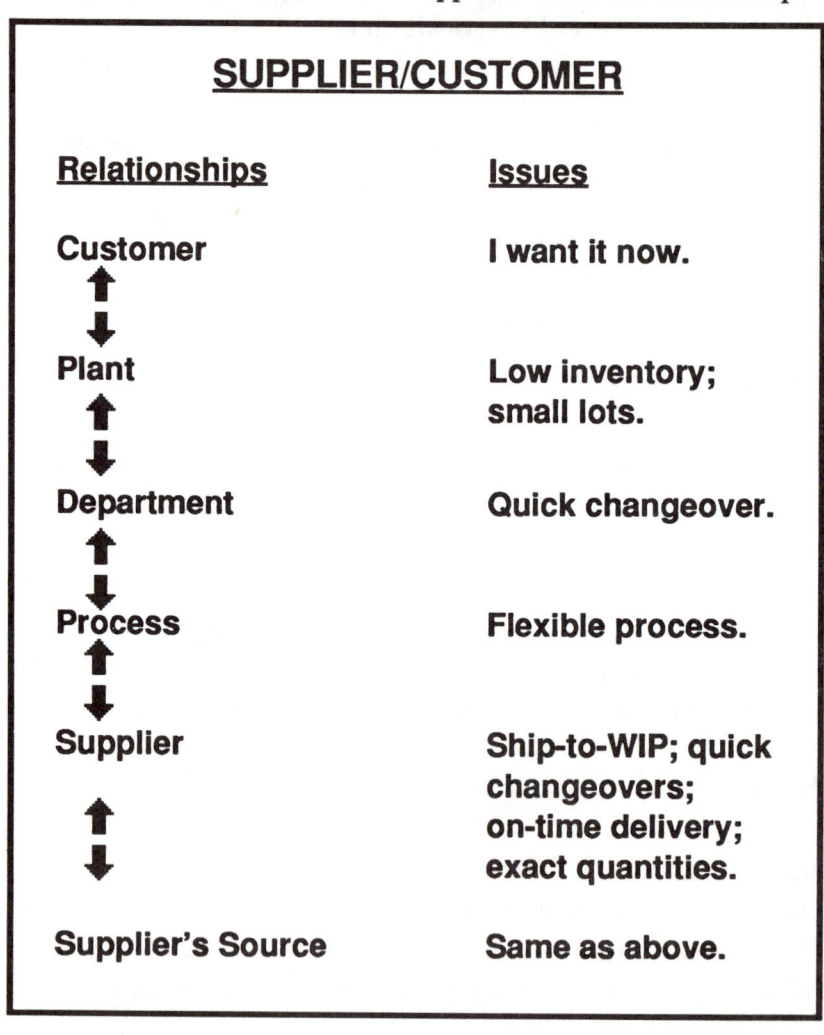

SUPPLIER/CUSTOMER

Relationships	Issues
Customer	I want it now.
Plant	Low inventory; small lots.
Department	Quick changeover.
Process	Flexible process.
Supplier	Ship-to-WIP; quick changeovers; on-time delivery; exact quantities.
Supplier's Source	Same as above.

When starting to implement a set-up reduction program, look at the internal and external areas at the same time. A good Supplier Certification program will include set-up reduction in its requirements. Internally, this will result in streamlining production operations, minimizing queues, reducing set-up times, simplifying product design, evolving toward ship-to-WIP (work-in-process) and working toward a lot size of one. These improvements eliminate waste and simplify material flow, thus reducing the number and complexity of tooling, equipment and processes. Ultimately, you will improve profits while developing the ability to respond quickly with reduced inventory.

Externally, a look at set-up reduction means eliminating the attitude that a large number of suppliers brings security in the form of a consistent flow of material. In reality, that approach will result in the need to establish numerous programs, one for each supplier. You end up with a supplier network which is out of control and likely to result in logistical nightmares. Now, instead of implementing a set-up program with one supplier, we have several programs, all of which are not equally capable.

With a reduced base of suppliers, a successful program is obtainable. The reduction in set-up time allows a supplier to deliver the right quantity of a quality product on-time because the operations of the company are geared to quick changeovers.

SUPPLIER RELATIONS

The fifties was an era of adversarial relations in which customers made demands upon suppliers without extensive consultation in order to build an understanding between the two parties. By the late seventies, however, customers began to notice that this relationship had serious shortcomings. It was never entirely clear who was supposed to do what and when. Companies didn't work together to solve problems. What we witnessed was a degradation of quality, delivery and overall performance.

Next came the eighties and the era of supplier contracts. This era also did little to develop a program to improve performance. Instead, contract administrators, or lawyers, were hired in procurement functions to review contracts so there would be no ambiguity about how customers would work with suppliers. The result was what has become known as the "battle of the forms" which never solved any problems. What this era still left out was continual contact with the supplier to work on building a partnership. Both sides spent little time in process improvement, cost reduction or value analysis, let alone set-up reduction.

Now in the nineties, some forty years later, we truly start to talk about an era of partnership. Finally, we begin to ask what we expect from a partner. We have discovered in our work with clients (in industries such as metal fabrication, food processing, cosmetics, pharmaceuticals, electronics etc.) from around the world that there are nine objectives customers want suppliers to meet if a partnership is to work:

- Reduce set-up times and lot sizes.
- Increase frequency of deliveries and make sure they are on time, 100 percent of the time.
- Provide only 100 percent acceptable materials.
- Eliminate waste in the plant.
- Develop inventory turn objectives that can be met together.

- Seek simplicity in solutions, tooling, fixtures and equipment.
- Work for continuous improvement.
- Communicate results and make them visible.
- Share savings with rewards.

This is the foundation upon which you will create a sense of teamwork with a supplier. At the same time these objectives are assimilated and become second nature through training programs and open discussion at the supplier, both sides should be guaranteeing a successful program by following the guidelines below:

THE SEVEN-STEP PLAN

1. Avoid studying a set-up reduction project to death.

2. Don't be satisfied with early successes (easy reductions in set-up time).

3. Don't get tangled up in techniques; get started now.

4. Strive for continuous improvements; 50 percent improvement at a time.

5. Post problems, goals, accomplishments and measurements where they are visible to all.

6. Document all steps of your current set-up process (videotape preferred).

7. Seek simplicity in solutions—no cost/low cost.

THE CELLULAR APPROACH

The second strategy in starting a set-up reduction program is the utilization of cells. The rationale behind cells is that a small work group can be more productive than a large department. So, instead of welding, fabricating and painting departments on the factory floor, consider putting a welder, a fabricator and a painter in one cell where they work as a unit to improve the process. This cell is then responsible for making the product, or sub-assembly, from beginning to end by finding ways to perform quick changeovers.

For example, one of our clients manufactures cookware. At the start, they found that it was not possible to go completely over to a cell approach. But, they did find that they could take one part of their production, the making of covers (which were standard), and cycle them through cells. The results were startling. What used to take 25 days is now done in four hours. In addition, one operation in the cell was able to talk to the preceding operation and solve problems while work was being performed. Before a company starts automatically switching over to a cell environment, we stress that it is important to review all processes beforehand. A company needs to examine closely the need for cells with respect to their application before devoting resources and time.

GROUP TECHNOLOGY
AND THE FLEXIBLE WORKER

In group technology, the strategy for companies is to take boring, repetitive jobs and rotate them among the members of a work group. For example, at an engine assembly plant, one worker may start the day putting pistons in the engine. He then may switch to putting engine heads on and then maybe to tuning the engine and setting the timing. Each job, as a result, becomes more interesting since it is not done over and over. Consequently, workers take more pride in their work and quality increases. As another consequence, well-trained workers are now better able to attack set-up reduction since they know how the different parts of a production process fit together.

These cross-trained workers required for group technology are also more flexible and, like flexible equipment, good for a company. We will discuss this worker flexibility in more detail in Chapter Six. With a set-up reduction program in full effect, you will find that you run only those machines which need to be run in order to produce parts to fill a customer order. This may mean that some workers are idle, but not if they are flexible workers. Such workers can move to another machine, work on reducing set-ups even further or just practice changeovers. In order to accomplish this, such workers must be properly educated and trained.

Both cells and group technology expose equipment imbalances, or bottlenecks. Teams can then be assigned to machines in order to reduce its set-up or process time so that it is in line with other equipment in the group. It may also require fine tuning of plant layouts. Toyota, for example, reformatted their entire plant layout five times in seven years. The company started with one person to one machine, then one person to two machines, and so on. On a recent fact-finding tour of the Far East, we observed one machine shop with hundreds of machines run by 13 skilled workers. We also saw another company where one cell of sixteen machines was run by a single person who did not perform any set-ups at all.

In the future, group technology will drive the set-up reduction program to the point where the need to changeover is completely eliminated. Most processes are either dedicated or flexible enough that a whole family of components can be manufactured. Thus, as Computer Aided Design (CAD) and Computer Assisted Manufacturing (CAM) become more prominent, we will find that products are designed so that no set-ups are required in the process. We will be able to go directly from the product design in the CAD system to control of the machine in the CAM system. Already, fixtures are being designed so that they are merely rotated to perform the next job. And that rotation is done at the instruction of the computer, not manually. It is important to realize that set-ups can be eliminated in the design stage when CAD/CAM is combined with group technology. It is more difficult to reduce set-up times if a process is put into place where set-ups have not been addressed in the design stage.

AUTOMATION AND ROBOTICS

Many companies have used the strategy of automating without first reducing set-up times and lot sizes. Such a strategy only nets a small improvement in run time and not a significant reduction in lead time. When using this strategy, we advocate following the Law of Judicious Utilization.

LAW OF JUDICIOUS UTILIZATION

Simple solutions are the best use of resources.
Only automate on a cost/benefit basis after other
alternatives have been exhausted.

With this law in mind, you would eliminate waste and then go out into your company and look at the following areas in which "judicious" automation can be effected:

- **Process.**
- **Equipment.**
- **Handling.**
- **Storage.**

Automation also applies to data flow. Bar coding speeds up the flow of information in a company by reducing the number of errors and the unnecessary set-up of data collection. Companies often use bar coding to assist in communicating the status of the flow and in enhancing the reliability of data collection.

Whatever the form of automation or robotics, we support its use. Automation assuredly has its place in a company's future. We're just advising you to use caution, not to fall into the "me too" trap. Use or buy automation only if you have a need for it, not because you heard about some other company who used or bought it. We recommend that you pay for automation out of the savings generated as a result of set-up reduction, lot size reduction and inventory reduction. This process forces the company to eliminate waste and then automate.

BENEFITS OF TOTAL COST JUSTIFICATION

The most effective way to stay out of the "me too" trap is to cost justify based on total cost. No company can expect to implement a set-up reduction program without convincing top management of its vital importance and long-term benefits. It also entails laying out the costs involved in getting the project started and maintaining it. The most practical way to obtain costs is to involve your Finance or Accounting departments in devising ways to capture the savings as they occur. The following should be considered in a set-up reduction program:

- **Capital equipment.**
- **Tooling requirements.**
- **Fixtures (new or modified).**
- **Education and training.**
- **Storage (inventory carrying costs).**
- **Team meetings.**
- **Automation.**
- **CAD/CAM.**
- **Time to market.**
- **Inventory turns.**
- **Customer satisfaction.**
- **People utilization.**
- **Machine utilization.**
- **Design for producibility.**

For a set-up reduction program to be successful, companies must measure and report actual results achieved versus planned. This sets the tone for the Continuous Improvement Process of the set-up program. In the next chapter, we will look at just those areas of opportunity in a company where it is possible to initiate improvements by way of set-up reduction.

CHAPTER FOUR

IDENTIFYING AREAS OF OPPORTUNITY

Once a corporation has embraced the continuous improvement mindset with a commitment, dedication and company culture which is conducive to change, it will significantly simplify the implementation of a set-up reduction program. Finding a way to channel the energy and good spirits which accompanies the beginning of any project or implementation is critical to success. Equally important is identifying where to establish a program and how to gain the support of people in the task of solving problems. More programs fail because well-intentioned, but muddled companies attack the first problem to come along and not the ones that can have the highest impact on the implementation process. It would be like starting out in tennis and taking on Arthur Ashe as your first opponent. We are sure that it's going to be difficult for a novice to win against him. You know all the strokes, how to serve and how to volley, but winning won't be easy against such a formidable opponent. The same lesson applies to set-up reduction. It may look courageous for you to attack the first problem that crops up or to go out and search for the most difficult problem, but it isn't the best strategy.

We have noticed many times that when we complete a two-day, internal, educational program in set-up reduction, the participants are like a bunch of football players in a locker room before a big game. They want to run out on the field and tackle something, anything. When we review the progress some weeks later, we discover that the company has accomplished few of the tasks it was all set to tackle. In reviewing the approach of many companies to the implementation of a set-up reduction program, we often find a lack of leadership, planning and direction. Many companies feel that when they educate the workers that the responsibility for the program's success has passed from management to direct labor.

These same companies, however, fail to realize the human issues involved. For example, there's the supervisor who has been working at the company for the last 25 years. His view is that he has been doing set-ups this way (and, by the way, correctly) for over 20 years and no young whippersnapper is going to come along and tell him that it is possible to further reduce set-up time. There is also the direct operator who views the whole set-up reduction program as just another obstacle in her way. They (meaning you, the company) are just making her job more difficult with all these new rules and reports.

We hope that you now realize that identifying the right area of opportunity is not as easy as it seems. The concerns of supervisors and operators need to be taken into consideration as well as financial and technical factors. Implementing set-up reduction requires support, not criticism, and the total endorsement of the program by management within the company.

We advocate that you put the odds in your favor when developing an area to begin set-up reduction. It's an opportunity for the program to prove itself against negative criticism and non-support. We must establish, learn and grow from these opportunities so that we can then establish set-up reduction as a Continuous Improvement Process.

In short, begin where you can get the "biggest bang for the buck." This does not necessarily mean the biggest return on investment. but if it does, that's an added benefit. Sometimes, however, a project that supports people's real needs may be "number one." By "biggest bang," we believe you should be looking for a high confidence area where you know good results can be achieved quickly, the proverbial "piece of cake." This proves the set-up reduction program to others in the company, whether the others are management or hourly labor. Nothing overcomes doubt and resistance like success. Look for an area which is going to give you a success right out of the starting block.

GATHERING DATA

It must be recognized that techniques of focused data gathering must be developed early in the program in order to conduct set-up reduction properly. Data gathering, in fact, is equally important in the selection of an area in which to begin as it is in the tracking of progress in set-up reduction. The following suggestions are intended to provide you with an idea of where to begin gathering information in the company. Collect data to determine:

- Critical work centers which are capacity limited at certain times during the week, month or year (seasonal peaks, holidays, etc.). While overall capacity may be in line with total customer demand, particular work centers can become overloaded and bottleneck the production flow. Production Planning is a good place to identify critical work centers.

- Work centers where large queues of inventory and dollars are tied up. Large queues are a visual indicator of bottleneck operations, excessive lot sizes and long set-up times. They are best located by walking out to the factory floor and observing. These areas, once found, provide a ripe opportunity to reduce lead time, throughput, inventory and to push for the theoretical lot size of one.

- Long changeovers or excessive down-time resulting in a significant loss of dollars. Often, this is the changeover which takes the longest time. Lowering total cost through the elimination of waste is a cornerstone of set-up reduction philosophy and practice.

- A major product line that carries the company financially or accounts for 80 percent of the company's volume. Other things being equal, it might be a good idea to start here first. The major product line probably offers a significant opportunity for profit improvement compared to other product lines. Following Pareto's law which says that 20 percent of the products and operations account for 80 percent of the dollar volume, this approach will maximize the program's "biggest bang for the buck." Additionally, a major, early payback will fund the program and help fan the fires of change.

- Interruptions in process and product flow. Follow products as they flow, or don't flow, throughout the plant to determine if this is an issue to confront. Interruptions may be costing the company a lot of money which should flow to profits. These areas are ideal places to employ the "Five Why" technique and other problem-solving techniques such as fishbone diagrams.

- Any areas with capacity constraints (bottlenecks). Use production planning and scheduling to help you with the collection of this information. Once collected, you many direct a set-up reduction team to help eliminate the constraint.

- Products which are never shipped on time. Ask your customers what products are the culprits and use their input to focus your effort on "why." The "why" may well be set-up time. Products which aren't shipped on time have a "snowball" effect on poor customer service. Total cost escalates as irate telephone calls increase and expediters are employed to stem the tide of customer order cancellations.

- Products where the time to market is long are one of the biggest concerns of marketing and sales. Sharpen your competitive edge in the world market of the 1990s by addressing set-up reduction in the product design phase.

Remember also to address the total product. It is of little value to reduce the set-up time for one component of a ten-component product, if the set-up times for the remaining nine components are not addressed as well.

- Look for areas where set-up personnel are working excess hours of overtime. Ask yourself what the benefit would be if quick change was in place. Charting or graphing overtime hours will very quickly highlight areas of capacity imbalances.

- If you find areas in which tool, fixture and die life is outside of normal ranges, find out if set-up reduction can solve the problem. Exploration in this area is intended to identify excessive run lengths, poor set-up and run procedures, inconsistent incoming materials and inadequate machine and die maintenance procedures.

- Any tooling which was ordered prior to two years before the established start date for the set-up program. These are always suspect areas because of non-standardization. Standard press/die shut heights, clamping positions, positive stops, one-touch fasteners are some of the many components of set-up reduction which have probably not been incorporated into older tooling. Therefore, they contribute to long changeovers. Examine tooling and standardize how it is installed, removed, clamped, etc.

- Excess material handling equipment, personnel and time spent on the movement of material. Material handling time is wasted money. It does not add value to the product. Lot sizes of one piece which are passed hand to hand or machine to machine are the ideal we must strive for.

- Work centers where bottlenecks occur are just like capacity constraints. If it happens a lot, it is the place to start.

- Areas in which large amounts of inventory sit idle offer an excellent opportunity for set-up reduction. By cutting set-up time by 50 to 75 percent, it is possible to reduce lot sizes by 50 to 75 percent. The average on-hand inventory and associated inventory carrying costs will plummet by a similar amount. And with reduced lead times, forecast inaccuracy is reduced, thus eliminating the need for excessive safety or buffer stocks.

- Missed deliveries is one of the larger areas of need because companies aren't flexible enough to ship on time, every time. Lead time needs to be what customers require, not what our current manufacturing and administrative practices tells us it has to be.

- Since set-up is the main contributor to long lead-time items, you should look at those items and assign them to a set-up reduction team for improvement.

- Finding the longest set-up times may be the easiest way to determine where to start. Find this area and you have probably found a "gold mine." It represents the greatest opportunity for set-up and associated lot size reductions. The order of magnitude of reductions in average inventory is much greater and represents the greatest potential savings.

- Areas where shelf life is an issue. Search out those areas where you are always giving credits. Shelf life issues indicate low inventory turnover rate and are very costly to you and your customers. Obviously, shorter set-up times and smaller lot sizes reduce on-hand inventory requirements and accelerate inventory turnover rates from "turns to spins."

- Stockouts represent the ultimate failure of your company to your customers. The application of set-up reduction improves flexibility in light of unplanned customer demand, thus reducing stockouts and the need for the "full wagon or shelf" theory of marketing.

- Customer satisfaction is your reward for success. If it ever drops off, that is an opportunity which must be addressed with quick changeovers.

- Competition in world market—look for products which are currently or will be targets for competition and aggressively reduce set-up time. It will be too late if the competition gets ahead of us.

- Another area of opportunity can be found by collecting data on machine up-time. You should report and track the amount of machine up-time for all the equipment on your production line. If there is an excessive amount of down-time, find out why. You will often discover that the reason has to do with the amount of time it takes to perform a set-up. Don't, however, be overly concerned with whether a machine is making parts or not. Be concerned instead with the machine's availability for process. This is not the amount of time the machine is running, but the amount of time it is available to run as compared to the amount of time it is in set-up or undergoing maintenance. Also, if you have true flexibility, then you have lot-for-lot production. Production, in other words, is driven by customer orders which means it would be unproductive to run a machine for which there are no orders.

THE NEED FOR FLEXIBILITY

An area that deserves special mention is the collection of data to determine where flexibility in manufacturing capability is most critical. The first rule in finding that area, which is in critical need of set-up reduction, is to listen to people, the people who work for the company or supply the company with products or who are the customers.

We have a client, for example, who believed its customers were not interested in whether the company could reduce lot sizes or work-in-process with a set-up program. This particular company manufactures album covers for the record industry. Their reasoning went like this: "We don't have to be flexible because our customers don't want flexibility. We make record covers by the thousands and they always order them by the thousands."

The first thing we asked our client was whether this was an assumption or a real demand. Or, was this the result of a practice which had become ingrained over time? They had to admit that they weren't sure, so we suggested that they ask their customers: "If you could receive less album covers and still get a fair cost, would you order less than the minimum lot of 5,000?"

Every one of them, to the person, said that they would. In fact, many said they would order as few as 500 album covers for works by new musicians or groups in order to test the product in selected markets whose business they didn't previously take on.

The lesson to be learned from this example is that managers and executives should review areas that identify why their company requires more flexible manufacturing. This will inevitably lead the company to each supporting work center which needs set-up reduction, since set-up reduction is the major driving force behind becoming more flexible. Remember to use a Different Set of Eyes (DSE). If set-up reduction is left only to Manufacturing to attack, results may not be as easily gained due to the Not Invented Here (NIH) syndrome.

TOTAL PRODUCT INVOLVEMENT

A key question that arises when a company is deciding where to begin its implementation of set-up reduction is determining how far to extend the program initially. Some companies break down their set-up reduction by part or process; other companies break down their program by machine. The latter is especially true in discrete environments where a particular machine changes frequently to produce different items. A company may also want to break down their set-up reduction program by an entire family of items. Perhaps there is an item group or a "bread and butter" family of products which generates the most customer orders or dollars affecting the plant. If so, start here with set-up reduction.

Companies may also find it advisable to group like items or items of similar complexity. The best way to find the areas in which this is possible is to talk with the engineers and programmers who work on Computer Aided Design (CAD) or Computer Aided Manufacturing (CAM) systems. Ask them if they could run other parts on a machine, if the machine was available and the set-up time had been reduced. They will often answer that there are many instances where other parts could be run, but they never were because the changeover took so long.

In the flexible manufacturing line at the Macintosh facility of Apple Computer, Peter Grieco states that as part of the design of the factory, tooling and material systems had to have minimized set-up times. In fact, set-ups had to be done in a matter of minutes. This is especially necessary for companies running high volumes of components as the Macintosh facility did. When companies begin with reduced set-up time, minimal material or process as the design objective, success comes far more easily.

TRANSFERABILITY ("CLONING")

We have discussed some of the criteria for selecting an area to begin set-up reduction. After an area has been determined to be of high priority, the next criterion is to determine whether the knowledge learned in one area can be transferred to other work centers in the company. Clearly, transferability is highly desirable in that it will greatly decrease the learning curve for other areas. Thus, a pilot area must have the potential to be a model application or test site for the company.

All procedures and methodologies should be rigorously documented or recorded in the pilot area so they can be standardized and transferred to other work areas. It is best to apply only proven techniques, methods and changes in order to guarantee continued success in the program. Videotapes of the improved set-up procedure with choreographed scripts are a great benefit at standardizing the "cloning" process.

USING PARETO CHARTS

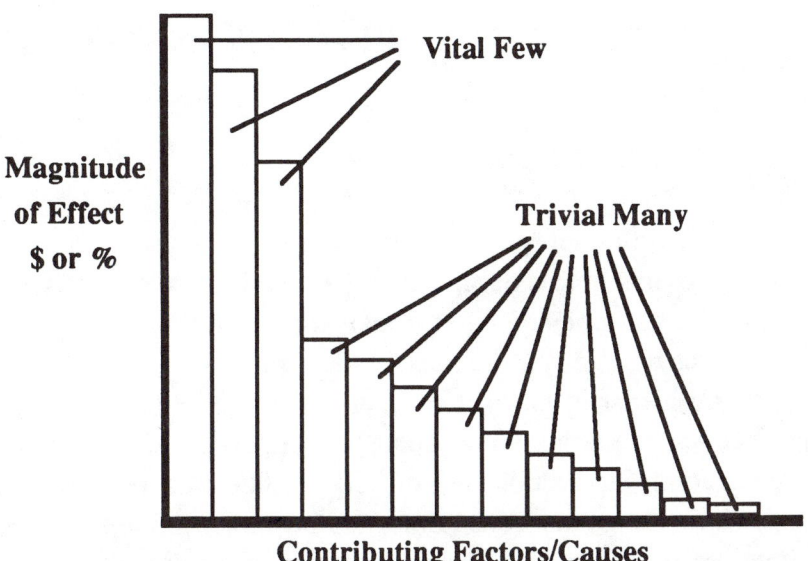

Contributing Factors/Causes

The purpose of gathering information in a pilot area is to avoid making fundamental mistakes in problem solving. A major mistake is to begin the solution process without first defining the problem. The critical step is to identify the specific problem using the information you have gathered and then to break the problem down into "bite-sized" pieces. Breaking the problem down is where a Pareto chart can assist.

A Pareto chart will help set priorities and show the relative importance of causes to each other and to the overall problem condition. Knowing this, a company can decide which problem to solve first. The chart on the previous page shows how the contributing factors or causes contribute to the problem.

Approximately 5 to 20 percent of the contributing factors (the vital few) account for 60 to 85 percent of the total effect. Obviously, then your first efforts should be aimed at the "vital few."

EXAMPLES OF SET-UP REDUCTION EFFORTS

TRINITY INDUSTRIES

Set-up reduction programs, while generally focusing on one machine or machine grouping at a time, need not be restrictive in scope. An example of an optional, more global view is that undertaken by Trinity Industries (headquartered in Dallas, Texas), the world leader in railroad car manufacturing. Historically, no project was too large, no product too complex for this "can do" organization. Production runs of 250 to 1,000 cars, on schedule and within budgetary constraints, had become routine business. However, management, with an eye toward future growth, began to identify an untapped market potential for orders totaling 25 to 50 cars.

The problem, really the opportunity, was to develop methods of set-up (quick line changeover) and enhanced manufacturing processes which would support small lot production, maintain high quality standards and meet per car total cost objectives.

"How do we direct out substantial resources to this complex task in the most efficient and timely manner?" was the question posed by Jerry Pennington, Manager of Manufacturing—Tank Car Division.

The answer, for Trinity, came in the form of a set-up reduction/ process improvement team which was focused at their Fort Worth, Texas facility. This group, consisting of representatives from a cross-section of functional areas, attacked the problem head on. They began by listing all of the various reasons why small lot production was infeasible. For example:

- **We have never done it this way before.**

- **Learning curves won't allow efficient production.**

- **The fixturing is too large, immobile and expensive.**

And so on and so on.

Armed with a prioritized "gloom and doom" list, Trinity set out to make small lot production work. Subscribing to the principle that "people who say it can be done and people who say it can't be done will both be right," the company's "can-do" attitude led them in only one direction—the Continuous Improvement Process.

To this day, the team is realizing substantial lead time and throughput improvements through concentration on such areas as:
- **Mobile sectional fixturing.**
- **Precision alignment guides.**

- One-touch/tool-less, hold-down devices.
- Precision "first time," fit-up positioning.
- Expanded automatic welding applications.

Trinity is succeeding primarily due to its company mind-set as expressed by Dan Banks, Vice President—Tank Car Division when he stated:

> *"Trinity is committed,*
> *through employee involvement,*
> *to the quest to be*
> *the highest quality and lowest cost producer*
> *in the industry."*

COSMAIR, INC.

Cosmair began the development of its flex line with the intention of eliminating set-up throughout its packaging operation. Cosmair's previous packaging line was the typical straight line which measured 20' x 85', or 1700 sq. ft. Eight to nine people were needed to run the line and all were doing repetitive, boring tasks. The straight line was flexible in the sense that a number of different kinds of packages could be run, but the line's changeover time was measured in hours. In addition, quality suffered because of the long conveying distances, the number of machines handling packages and the number of manual operations. Quality inspection was also done off-line and not by the operating crew.

Cosmair set out to reduce the changeover time and to improve quality. Their solution was to incorporate set-up reduction techniques with the most innovative packaging equipment into a production area which they call the flex line. The new line is in an efficient, U-shaped layout of 30' x 40', or 1200 sq. ft., a savings of 500 sq. ft. Only one operator and a small crew of packers is needed to run the entire line. The operator, besides running the machines, is also responsible for:

- **Planning.**   • **Problem-solving.**
            • **Productivity measurement.**

In other words, Cosmair introduced the concept of the Continuous Improvement Process into the design of the line. This concept is reinforced by the addition of a meeting area with a drawing board where team members can solve problems.

Product design features were also taken into consideration. The flex line is able to handle all of the containers and packages with no changeovers. Robots are programmed so that all possible package configurations are stored in their memories. Thus, changeover only requires the push of a button. Equipment design changes were incorporated into the line as well. The filling unit, for example, is now designed so that an alternate filling nozzle can be set up and calibrated while the filler is running. The flex line also brought about improvements in quality by:

- **Shortening conveying distances.**
- **Reducing handling of packages.**
- **Introducing precision product filling
  and cap torquing.**

The result: Whereas changeover time used to be measured in hours, it can now be done in less than 10 minutes.

WORK CELL DEVELOPMENT

Most companies have all the data needed to identify areas of opportunity. Sometimes all it takes is asking the employees for input in establishing work cells, or teams, to look for the data. Make sure that when teams are developed that they have a uniform selection criteria for evaluating opportunities. All teams should evaluate initial opportunities based upon their "potential for success" and their maximization of savings. All opportunities which pass these initial tests should then be ranked on the basis of a descending cost/benefit analysis.

Where you start depends upon your specific needs. Review this chapter when you begin to determine your greatest area of need and then start there. Start where you will have the greatest benefit. Set-up reduction teams will greatly aid you in this determination. Let's now turn our attention to the next two chapters to see just how teams develop and work in a set-up reduction program.

CHAPTER FIVE

ORGANIZING
A SET-UP REDUCTION TEAM
FOR RESULTS

Once a company identifies a problem through an analysis of the data which has been collected, it must direct the set-up reduction team to seek solutions. Over the years, we have developed a four-step problem-solving process. We recommend the four-step process in all cases except those which involve low-cost/no-cost solutions where it is more effective simply to implement the solution.

PROBLEM-SOLVING TECHNIQUES

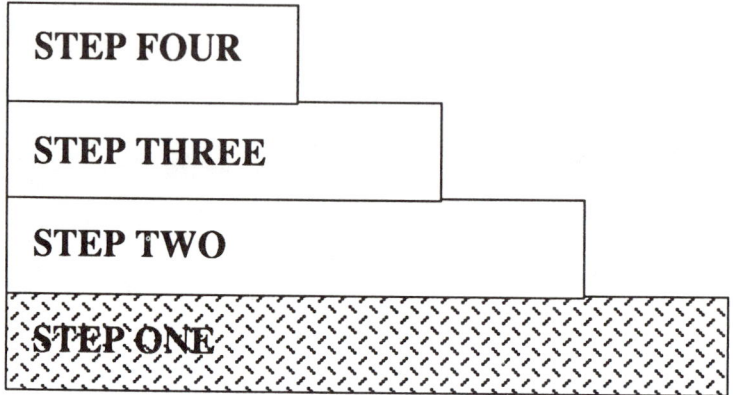

Step One: NAME THE PROBLEM

The first step for the set-up reduction team is to use the form in Figure 1 which is divided into three columns with the following headings:

- **Symptoms.**
- **Possible causes.**
- **Verified root causes.**

In the first column, the team writes down the symptom from which the company is suffering and that they will attempt to remedy. The key element here is that what we formerly labeled a problem was in reality a symptom. Examples are late deliveries of tools, part shortages, line-up problems, maintenance problems, etc. Symptoms consist of many causes, each of which is a problem to be solved by the group once it is verified.

Symptom	Possible Causes	Verified Root Causes
Set-up personnel not using the same procedure on all 3 shifts. Therefore the time to change over is uncontrollable.		

Figure 1

In the second column, the team lists all of the possible reasons why a particular symptom could be occurring. This is shown in Figure 2 on the next page. These two columns should be able to be completed in a one-hour meeting.

Filling in the third column (Figure 3), in which the team must decide what are the vital few, or root causes, is the most difficult part. The team must find the two or three causes which would make most of the symptoms disappear if those causes were attacked and solved. This stage can require as little as a week or

Symptom	Possible Causes	Verified Root Causes
	1. Worker attitude	
	2. Lack of understanding	
	3. Supervisor direction	
	4. Lack of training	
	5. Length of time on job	
	6. Maintenance of equipment	
	7. Complexity of changeover	
	8. Operator direction	
	9. Lack of proper tools	
	10.) Lack of inspection tools	
	11. Lack of documented specs	
	12. Process not capable	

Figure 2

month to complete, depending on the time alloted to problem-solving. The team leader must make assignments for each possible cause indicated in the second column. Team members then have to go out and do research on the factory floor and wherever else to collect data and talk to the people who are involved. Then, the team members are expected to come back to the meeting and compare data. This process must continue until they are able to identify three root causes.

Symptom	Possible Causes	Verified Root Causes
		1. Lack of training 2. Maintenance of equipment

Figure 3

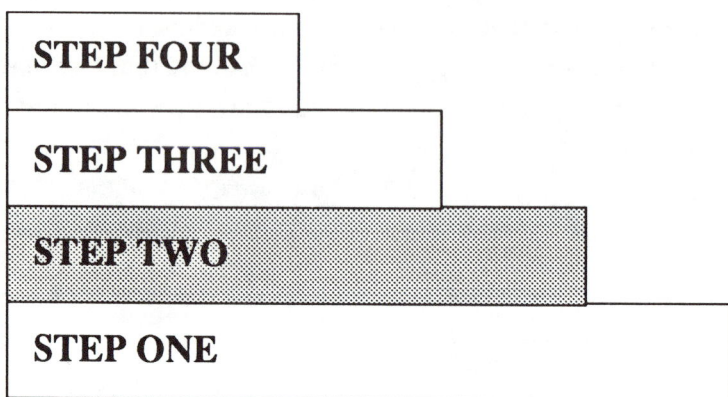

Step Two: FIND A WAY

Next the team must find *ways* to *eliminate* each of these root causes. The key words here are "ways" and "eliminate." We need to look beyond the first solution which comes to mind and we must be sure that each solution positively "kills" the problem. This process is known as "killing snakes" at Trinity Industries, Inc. Daryl Collins, the production control manager, was instrumental in using this process to identify and eliminate the root causes of poor schedule attainment. By finding ways to eliminate lack of material, machinery breakdowns, etc., Trinity was able to attain levels of 90 to 100 percent performance to schedule at several locations. This process begins when the team leader fills out the form on the next page for each problem, or Verified Root Cause.

Then the leader points to the first problem, Verified Root Cause #1, and asks the team members for potential ways to eliminate the problem. The leader then directs a discussion of each possible solution. He or she does not list a second solution until the team is reasonably sure that the first solution will work.

MUST FIND **WAYS** TO **ELIMINATE**	
_____ (Verified Root Cause)	

	Cost of Each Solution
Solution #1: _____ _____ _____	#1
Solution #2: _____ _____ _____	#2
Solution #3: _____ _____ _____	#3
Solution #4: _____ _____ _____	#4
Solution #5: _____ _____ _____	#5

NEXT STEP = EXECUTE

WHO _____   **WHEN** _____

_____   _____

_____   _____

The first solution will often suggest that the company either spend money, buy equipment or hire people. The second solution is the hardest one to come up with. Many companies have not evolved the process to a level which is imaginative enough to go beyond the first solution. When a second solution has been put forward, the leader does not ask for a third solution until the team is, once again, reasonably sure that Solution #2 will eliminate the root cause. The leader continues this same procedure for the third, fourth and fifth solutions. We recommend five solutions as a rule of thumb, but don't force five if there are only four solutions. Don't study a problem to death. Likewise, don't stop at five, if more solutions come easily.

```
┌─────────────────────────┐
│   STEP FOUR             │
├─────────────────────────┴───────┐
│   STEP THREE                    │
├─────────────────────────────────┴───────┐
│   STEP TWO                               │
├──────────────────────────────────────────┴───────┐
│   STEP ONE                                        │
└───────────────────────────────────────────────────┘
```

Step Three: ASSIGN COSTS

Step three is relatively straight-forward. Take each of the solutions for a particular root cause and assign a cost to it in terms of people, machines and materials. Put this dollar amount in the appropriate space on the form on the previous page. After this is done, it is obvious which solution to implement—the one with the *lowest cost* since the team is already reasonably sure that all the solutions will solve the problem.

| STEP FOUR |
| STEP THREE |
| STEP TWO |
| STEP ONE |

Step Four: EXECUTE THE PLAN

From our experience, we have found it necessary to add an execution step to this problem-solving technique. Sometimes, teams believe that going through the three previous steps automatically makes the problem disappear. Or, they believe that their job is finished and now it is up to someone else to implement the solution. We advocate that the team be given the *responsibility* and *authority* to implement its own solutions. If the problem doesn't go away, then the team did not implement the solution properly and must try again to solve the problem.

This four-step process can also be used to develop a presentation to top management. Now a team can say: We've looked at the symptoms. We identified these possible causes and then we verified these three as the roots of the problem. We've come up with five ways to eliminate each problem. This is the one with the lowest cost. This is the one we are going to implement."

Does this problem-solving process work? We've been involved in many instances where it absolutely does. At one foundry, we facilitated a set-up team tackling the problem of air trapped in castings. The company was currently scrapping three castings (roughly 8' x 4' x 4') per month. The team went through the steps above and came up with six solutions. The first cost $100,000. The sixth cost $150 per year. Was it good a solution? It was good enough so that in the last nine months, the company has not scrapped any castings. Did the team "kill" the problem? Yes, absolutely.

FISHBONE DIAGRAMS

Tom Peters, at a recent talk, told the assembled businesspeople that if companies did not know how to do fishbone diagrams by 1991, they would be educationally deficient. Fishbones are tremendous brainstorming tools. We particularly recommend using them when it is not possible to take a videotape of a set-up being performed. We also advise clients to put the fishbone diagram on a "wipe-off" board in the work area. Then, people can list possible causes underneath each category. We do ask that people put their name down in case the team has more questions to ask. Another way is to make one list of all the causes and then categorize each item under the six headings.

As the cause and effect (fishbone) diagram on the next page shows, the intent is to identify a problem and its possible causes and then to note which causes are being worked on and which are done. We tell teams to put parentheses "( )" around what the team is currently working on and to erase the parentheses and put a dot next to the item when it is finished. This makes the diagram a great

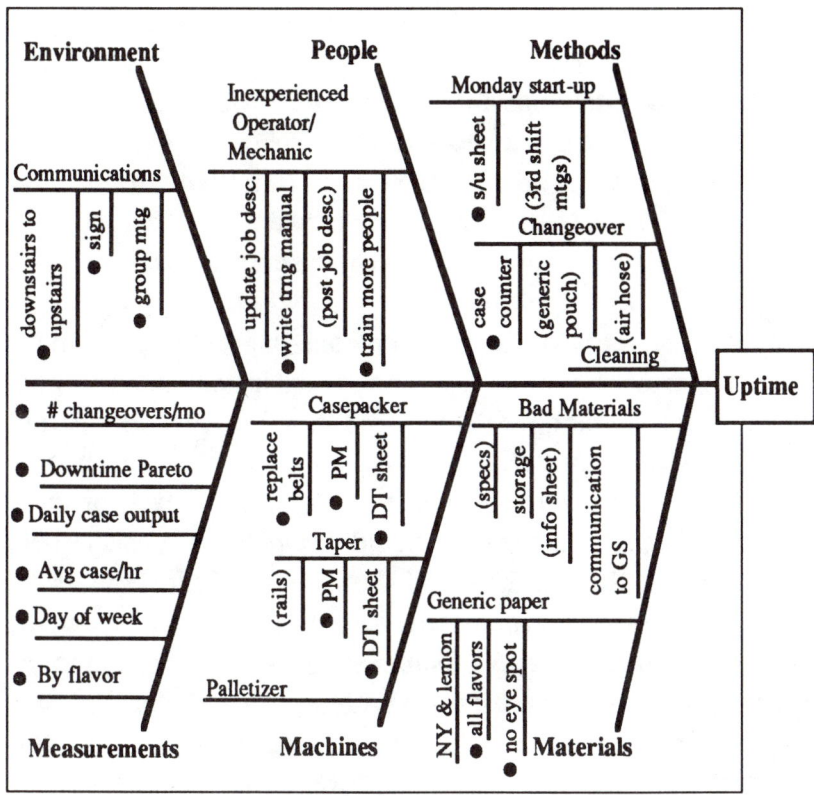

Fishbone Diagram

visual reminder of progress as well as an indicator of what specific cause they are working on at the moment.

One variation on the fishbone idea is to put the diagram on a 4' x 8' sheet of board. Other employees are encouraged to add possible causes, not identified by the team, by sticking "post-it" notes on the board under the appropriate heading. It is very possible that the person with the ideal solution is not a team member. This method allows that person to make a contribution.

Fishbones are also valuable for the following reasons:

- **Identify possible causes of a problem.**
- **Relate causes to effects.**
- **Analyze all possible causes of a problem.**
- **Trace the symptoms of causes.**
- **Break problems into their smallest parts.**

Fishbone diagrams make excellent one-page memos. Send a diagram like the above and top management instantly knows what is being done. In fact, we recommend that fishbones be a part of the ten-minute presentations that set-up reduction teams should make to the steering committee every month. In each of these presentations, the team leader should first put up a measurement graph and talk about it. It should show, for example, how set-up time has decreased (or increased) over the past month. Then, the team leader should put up a fishbone diagram and explain to the steering committee what the team is doing now and what has been completed. Lastly, the team leader should tell the committee how the team went through the four-step process for problem-solving in order to get viable solutions. This makes a far more effective presentation than someone reading the minutes of the previous month's meetings as well as being much more efficient and timely.

PROBLEM-SOLVING CHECKLISTS

The following six checklists will help a company begin the problem-solving process necessary for a successful set-up reduction program.

CHECKLIST #1: MATERIAL

Use of better materials, or use of present materials in more efficient ways, can greatly improve set-up time.

___ Could a less expensive material be used which would function as well?

___ Does the material arrive at the work center in suitable condition for use?

___ Could the supplier or previous work center do additional work on the material to make it better suited for use?

___ Is the material clean enough for use?

___ Is the material ordered in quantities or sizes that facilitate the most efficient use of set-up time?

___ Would a more expensive material, which was easier to process, result in a saving?

___ Can the product design be changed to eliminate material requiring lengthy or costly set-ups?

___ Is it possible to reduce the number of materials by standardizing product designs?

___ Are provisions in place for segregation of different material cuttings to assure maximum return?

__ If a more consistent grade of material was used, would it be possible to gain better control of set-up operations necessary for processing the material?

CHECKLIST #2: MATERIAL HANDLING

Material handling is not only the movement of material from work center to work center. It includes the movement of material at the work center as well. Better material handling can improve housekeeping, simplify operations and improve quality, all of which will greatly impact set-up reduction.

__ Should operators perform material handling functions?

__ Should special racks or trays be developed to improve handling time and to decrease the amount of damage done to material?

__ With respect to the work center, where should incoming and outgoing material be located?

__ Can work centers which do successive steps of the process be moved closer together to improve material handling?

__ Is the size of the container which is used to transport material suitable for the size or quantity of material needed?

__ Can the container be designed to make the material more accessible?

__ Can material be handled during an idle period of the operation?

__ Is the storage area efficiently located?

__ Can waist-high material containers be used at work centers?

__ Is it possible to combine operations at a work center to reduce material handling?

CHECKLIST #3: SET-UP AND PUT AWAY

This checklist focuses on the set-up person or the operator if he or she performs the set-up as well.

__ How is the job assigned to the operator?

__ What possibilities for delays occur at the storeroom?

__ If the operator performs the set-up, would there be any gains if it was done by a trained set-up person?

__ Is the work center orderly so that tools can be found quickly?

__ Are the tools used in the set-up adequate?

___ Is the machine in proper working condition?

___ Is the workplace layout an effective one? Or, can a more efficient way be found to arrange work centers?

___ Is the material properly positioned?

___ Are the first few pieces produced checked by anyone other than the operator?

___ How is the material supply replenished?

___ If a number of miscellaneous jobs are done, can they be grouped together to eliminate some set-up elements?

___ Are benches and tables of the proper height and design?

___ Who checks the fluid levels of the equipment and performs other preventive maintenance?

___ Are tools transferred from one shift or worker to another without undue loss of time?

___ Could guides be used to position parts more accurately?

___ Do all operators and set-up people use the same tools?

___ Do all operators and set-up people use the same procedure?

___ Are proper measuring instruments provided for precision work and are they calibrated on a regular schedule?

___ Would it be feasible to hang tools on springs overhead?

___ Does the set-up person need to reach and could this distance be shortened?

___ Does the set-up person need to walk away from the work center? Could this be eliminated?

___ Will ratchet, spiral or power tools save time?

CHECKLIST #4: MACHINERY

___ Are machines checked on a regular schedule to insure good condition?

___ Are machines properly powered with the right type of motor?

___ Is this particular machine best suited to the job at hand?

___ Could the machine be outfitted or adapted to perform better or to allow for easier changeover?

CHECKLIST #5: WORKING CONDITIONS

Although not only a set-up issue, working conditions are serious deterrents to the performance of set-ups. Eliminating bad conditions can help reduce set-up time or work in correlation with other factors to reduce time.

___ Is lighting uniform and sufficient at all times?

___ Have glare and reflections been eliminated at the work center?

___ Is the proper temperature maintained for maximum productivity?

___ Is ventilation good?

___ Are safety factors duly emphasized?

___ Are tools and motor drives properly guarded?

___ Is wooden equipment, such as work benches, in good condition and free of splinters?

___ Is the floor free of debris and smooth, but not slippery?

___ Is the set-up person's clothing safe?

___ Can noisy conditions be quieted?

___ Is the area clean?

CHECKLIST #6: SHOP PRACTICES

__ Are adequate performance records maintained?

__ Are new set-up people properly introduced to their surroundings and are sufficient instructions given to them?

__ Are failures to meet standard performance requirements investigated?

__ Are suggestions from workers encouraged?

__ Is the set-up being performed by the proper class of labor?

__ Is the set-up person physically suited for the job?

PREVENTIVE MAINTENANCE AND THE SET-UP REDUCTION PROCESS

Most teams focusing on set-up reduction fail to pay enough attention to preventive maintenance. Many of the problems which set-up teams encounter as they view videotapes and study people performing changeovers are problems with the maintenance of the equipment. Predictive and preventive maintenance is, in many instances, important to the success or failure of a set-up reduction program.

Preventive maintenance basically insures that any equipment

used in the manufacturing of a product will be in full operating condition each and every time it needs to be used. The job of a Maintenance Department is to uncover maintenance problems before they interfere with set-ups. Its goal is to be proactive, instead of reactive, to approach a level where all problems can be predicted and will be prevented. The major tool which a Maintenance Department can use to reach this level is the gathering of data on equipment in order to perform a *mean time between failure analysis.*

Often, however, management is not concerned enough with preventive maintenance. Instead of finding ways to prevent outbreaks of problems, they spend a majority of their time putting out the fires caused by maintenance problems. Management should be alerted to the benefits of preventive maintenance and why it is vital to the success of a set-up reduction program. We have found that companies can achieve the following results from a preventive maintenance program:

- **Increased machine availability.**
- **Reduced spare parts inventory.**
- **Improved planning and execution of maintenance work orders.**
- **More efficient planning for turnarounds and shutdowns.**
- **Faster response to emergency work.**
- **Higher return on investments.**
- **Smoother maintenance scheduling.**
- **Lower total cost.**
- **Less downtime.**
- **Increased equipment life.**
- **Improved quality.**

As for emergency repairs, we believe that this is a critical area to measure in order to see how well a preventive maintenance program is working. Keep in mind, however, that in the short and intermediate term not all emergencies can be eliminated. It is possible to prevent 80 percent of them. When this is the case, it is possible to respond more quickly and efficiently to the emergencies which occur in the remaining 20 percent of the time because everything is not a "red-hot" emergency.

Some companies have gone out and purchased computer systems to record and track maintenance issues. This is worthless if nobody takes the recorded data, analyzes it and takes corrective action. Unfortunately, many companies go merrily along collecting information that they never use to improve themselves. We advocate that you take these maintenance records (whether done with a computer or manually) and form a preventive maintenance team to improve this area. An analysis of all the breakdowns on every work center for the past six months must be completed. Are there any identifiable patterns? Does anything keep recurring? Chances are that a team will see something like "adjust, adjust, adjust, replace" in the records. That's a clear indication that the tool or die may need replacing earlier or replaced so that a set-up person or operator doesn't need to run around looking for a replacement in the middle of a big job. By carefully analyzing the maintenance records, we can avoid this situation.

Companies that do preventive maintenance find that the following are true:

- **Equipment performs better.**
- **Equipment is more dependable.**
- **Equipment is able to hold tolerances better.**
- **Equipment is more valuable.**

In addition to the above, companies find that the resale value of their equipment is much greater if it is well maintained. We remember going to an auction where a 600-ton press was for sale. It was 30 years old, but except for some worn off paint, it looked immaculate. We looked at the maintenance records and saw why. The company selling the press had performed preventive maintenance for each of those 30 years. Not surprisingly, the machinery was selling for within $10,000 of a brand new press. And it was sold, quickly.

Peter L. Grieco, Jr, says that on a recent trip to The Toyota Engine Plant in Japan, he saw equipment that was maintained so well that it was in original working order. Most of the equipment was twenty years old, but looked brand new. Ironically, a large percentage of the equipment which they use to build their cars is made in America. American companies have to learn that they can't sacrifice preventive maintenance. It must be given top priority.

HOW TO ESTABLISH
PREVENTIVE MAINTENANCE

Most companies want to know how to establish a preventive maintenance program if they have not been collecting data or keeping records at all which is not an unusual case. We advise these people that they must begin collecting data right away. Set up a recordkeeping system. Devise a form which you can give to the Maintenance Department when there are problems. Keep data and flip charts by the work center. And most importantly, designate a person to collect the data and enter it into a computer system or into manually kept files.

Once data collection is established, don't wait a year before you look at the accumulated information. After three months, take a look. See if the data is telling you something about set-up problems. If it is, solve the problem. If it isn't, put the data away and look at it again at the end of six months. A word of caution: Don't overkill when doing preventive maintenance. It is just as wasteful to replace belts and bearings every three months even though it can be done once a year as it is not to replace them at all and wait for them to wear out. At one of our clients in the Mid-East oil industry, millions of dollars were being wasted on redundant equipment and early replacement due to an inadequate predictive data analysis and application.

When establishing preventive maintenance as part of your set-up reduction program, make certain that you include the operators of the machinery as the first line of defense. It is very easy for an operator to check fluid levels, for example, of oil, water or hydraulic fluid. We recommend providing your operators with an easy-to-follow checklist which keeps words to a minimum and relies on well-known symbols. For example, put a picture of a oil can on a form such as the one on the next page to remind an operator to check the oil level. If you put an acetate sheet over this form, the operator merely has to "x" the picture to indicate that it has been done. This is so easy to do, but that does not mean it gets done. We visited a company that has one maintenance person whose job it is to check the oil level in all the plant's machinery. The machinery is spread over seven buildings on eight acres of land. One day, we were accompanying him on his rounds. In one of the buildings, he checked the oil level at a machine and announced that he had got there *just in time*. The machine was almost out of oil.

PREVENTIVE MAINTENANCE CHECKLIST					
	Mon	**Tues**	**Wed**	**Thurs**	**Fri**
Water	✓			✓	
Oil	✓		✓		✓
Hydraulic		✓		✓	

He didn't get there just in time. He got there a little too late. Perhaps he avoided the machine completely breaking down, but what about all the wear and tear on the machine as it operated at less than optimal levels of oil. Our point is that this would not happen if the operator was in charge of maintaining his or her machine in a condition where it is always ready to be run at peak efficiency. A technique we recommend is to give the machine a fresh paint job and put a sign on it which says:

```
THIS MACHINE
MANAGED AND MAINTAINED
BY (OPERATOR'S NAME).
```

What better way to highlight responsiblity than through personal pride?

When a machine needs repairs or maintenance beyond the capability of the operator, companies must make sure that the Maintenance Department is given time to do its work. At a client company, a videotape of the set-up showed that the first three parts after each changeover always had to be scrapped because they were covered by oil. We were told by the management of that company that they could not figure out how to eliminate the problem. It was just something they had to live with. It was obvious to the set-up team that the material being stamped on this machine was soaking up the excess oil that accumulated while the die was in storage. By the fourth part, all the accumulated oil in the die that was coming from leaking hydraulic lines on the machine had been soaked up. The team saw that this was clearly a maintenance issue.

We discussed the problem with the Maintenance Department. How long would it take to fix this machine? Four hours, we were told. Why haven't you fixed it then? We can't get four hours to work on the machine. So, we walked over to Production Scheduling and asked if we could get four hours of downtime for that machine so it could be fixed? After some deliberation, Scheduling agreed to our request. We told Maintenance and the machine got fixed. Now it makes good parts right from the beginning and the costs of fixing the machine and the downtime are more than offset by the $5.25 saved for each part that is not scrapped.

Still another example of how important maintenance is to set-up reduction can be seen in the following example. At another client, we were videotaping a set-up on a press. The set-up person activated the machine to lower the press, but instead of cycling all the way down, it stopped at six inches and cycled back up. While the tape was running, the set-up person turned to the camera and said that that had never happened before. We said to keep on going and that we would discuss it later. When we were finished with the videotaping we went to the Maintenance Department and showed them what had happened. Has this ever happened before? You bet it had. Maintenance had seven reports of that problem, reported on different shifts by different set-up people. Again, if maintenance records were being analyzed with respect to set-ups, this situation could probably have been avoided.

SETTING THE STAGE
FOR EMPLOYEE INVOLVEMENT

It should be clear by now that set-up teams armed with problem-solving techniques are the most effective way to reduce set-up times and other problems, such as poor maintenance, which contribute to inefficiency. Technical knowledge is valuable and necessary, but, as we will see in the next chapter, so is the ability to get the best out of people by building a creative environment. Each part of the set-up reduction program is as critical as any other part. People issues need to be addressed. If they aren't, all the problem-solving techniques in the world won't help a team.

CHAPTER SIX

EMPLOYEE INVOLVEMENT

In a very real sense, set-up reduction is not a program for management alone. There is little chance of success if a company hands the program down from the ivory tower of management to the workers on the floor. A set-up reduction program demands that you recognize the importance of employees, that you give them the responsibility and authority to act on their own to further the company's objectives. If you fail to treat them with high regard, your primary source of new and creative ideas and solutions to problems will dry up like a lake in a desert. Fortunately, being creative is one of the most enjoyable activities at any person's job. Thus, getting employees involved in a set-up reduction program requires no more from management than allowing people the time and means to express their natural abilities, to be creative, to find solutions, to work as a team in a non-threatening environment. We must overcome those past feelings of mistrust which have kept people from expressing their natural creativity.

REWARDS AND INCENTIVES

It doesn't hurt, of course, to add some rewards and incentives to unleash people's natural tendency to want to improve their performance. Since a set-up program has an easily identifiable way of measuring progress, rewards can be linked to the amount of reduction in the set-up time for a machine as well as the amount of savings which have been generated by the shorter set-up time. What form these rewards and incentives take varies from company to company, but every company should reward its people as they have successes.

We know that we have to reward people if they put an extra effort into a set-up program, but companies often get confused about what motivates people. We believe people in a company are motivated by four factors:

HAVING FUN
RECOGNITION FOR A JOB WELL DONE
SATISFACTION FROM CONTRIBUTING TO THE COMPANY
MONEY—PAY FOR PERFORMANCE

Therefore, potential rewards and incentives can include all or some of the following:

- **Recognition Awards—Plaques, rings, trophies, certificates, etc. (see sample below)**

- **Shared Savings—A set percentage of all set-up related cost savings.**

- **Perks to employees—Trips, parking privileges, dinners, use of company vehicles, etc.**

Don't forget to ask your employees how they would like to rewarded. You may be surprised. You will find that they want recognition which is frequent and specific. Tell them that they did

This Certificate

is presented to

Production Scheduling

By _____

due to successful completion
of a 50% reduction in set-up time

on _____

presented
this _____ *day of* _____ *19* __

_____
_____
_____
_____

Set-Up Reduction Team   *Production Scheduler* a good job on a specific task or recognize them for cutting the set-up time in half. Don't just say, "Oh boy. That's great!" Tie it to something real and tangible, perhaps a measurement graph. Then you can say, "Look at that graph. This set-up used to take eight hours. Now we can do it in 10 minutes. Great job!"

Our general rule on rewards is that if you can share in the savings, do so. If you can't, or decide not to, then at least recognize people for their effort in the company newsletter or in a memo. Some companies have even put notices in their local newspaper about an employee's efforts so that the worker's friends, neighbors and family will know. If you give perks, remember that they don't necessarily have to be worth large amounts of money. Have your company's executives give up their parking spaces and give them to team members for a set amount of time. Give away football, baseball or theater tickets. Give employees chits redeemable at the company store for company products or a gift certificate at a local restaurant or department store. Be creative.

EMPLOYEE SUGGESTION PROGRAMS

Another way to reward people is to set up an employee suggestion program where a set amount of money is awarded for every suggestion. If you decide to do this, make sure that what constitutes a suggestion is clearly defined. Above all, make it clear that a complaint is not a suggestion. Tell your people that a suggestion should be in this format:

- **State the problem or issue.**

- **State how you think it could be solved or addressed.**

A Reward for a Suggestion

The best run companies in America are willing to follow through on ideas, to make "mistakes," because they know that only through experimentation will a company grow. These companies create an environment where it is safe to make suggestions. No suggestion, no question is unimportant. Toyota Motor Corporation, for example, has developed a suggestion system in which its non-management work force of 55,000 contributed over 2.5 million improvement proposals in a recent year. The Mazda Company recently received 350,000 suggestions from one plant of 800 employees. Obviously, it is safe to suggest changes at these companies.

SURVIVAL AS A MOTIVATING FACTOR

One of the strongest motivators for making a set-up program successful exists when a company's survival depends upon reducing costs. Needless to say, a company should never use survival as an incentive if it isn't true. We started working with a client, however, whose survival was at stake. The bank had already informed this $15 million manufacturer of Computer Numerically Controlled (CNC) woodworking machine tools that they would have to sell the company. It had lost money for the last three years. The workers were understandably concerned about their jobs.

We were invited to come into this company and assist them in implementing a set-up reduction program. At the end of the first year, this company was able to generate tangible, documented savings of $150,000. Management then went to the steering committee (which consisted of the president, some top management, middle management, supervisors and four direct laborers) and asked about the allocation of the savings. Instead of putting everything toward the bottom line, the steering committee decided to take one-third of the savings, $50,000, and distribute it equally among all of the employees. The reasoning was that everybody helped to make these savings happen and everybody should share in the tangible benefits.

THE RESULT

The company has now turned around and started making a profit. Once the employees saw that the company really meant that savings would be shared, progress in getting still more out of the set-up reduction program was remarkable.

THE ONE-HALF RULE

There are as many different ways to divide savings as there are companies. We have seen some who use the "1/2 Principle," in which one-half of the savings go to the bottom line and one-half to the set-up reduction program.

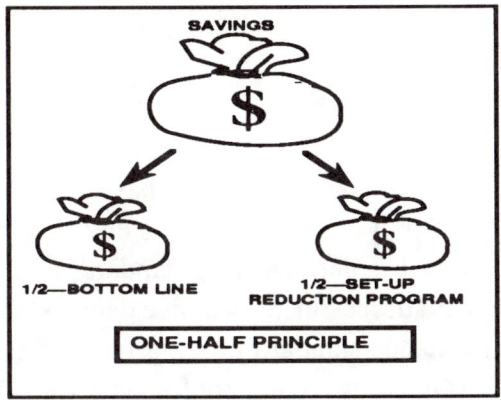

Others use the "1/3 Principle," in which one-third goes to the bottom line, one-third to the set-up program and one-third to the employees.

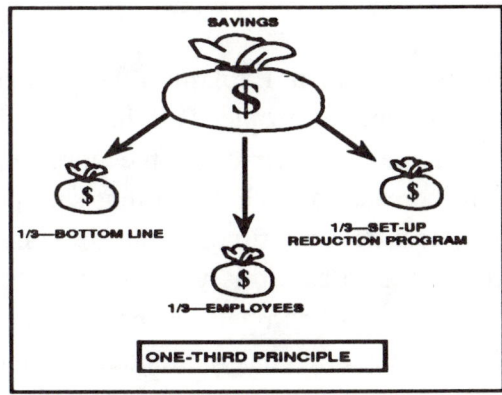

Still another popular way of dividing savings is to direct 45 percent to the bottom line, 45 percent to the set-up program and 10 percent to employees. Money given back to the program is used to buy equipment, tools, or material which will improve set-up times or to enhance education and training in set-up reduction so that even more savings can be generated. In other words, the program can begin to pay for its own growth out of its demonstrated performance.

INCENTIVE PLANS

Incentive plans at companies are often based on seniority, rather than what the employee knows. In this environment, it can be difficult to establish a performance standard, especially if your set-up program is successful. Successive decreases in set-up time keep the performance standard moving in the right direction—downward. This not only creates confusion about which standard is the correct one, but it can create resentment. If management tells employees that they are looking for one-third more capacity as a result of a set-up reduction program, many workers will interpret that as a requirement to work one-third harder or that one-third of their jobs will be cut.

Don't allow this to happen. Explain to the workers that you are going to cut jobs, but not people. Tell them that the company is doing set-up reduction in order to become more flexible so that the company can increase sales. Explain that set-up reduction improves quality and delivery times while decreasing the pricing cost base. Needless to say, this will make the company more competitive and the more competitive the company is, the more it has to produce. The more it has to produce, the more work there is for the people who presently work for the company. Market share expansion is an integral part of the strategy to attain "World Class Manufacturing." The success of the Japanese in the automotive and consumer electronics markets are ideal examples of the validity of this approach.

Getting back to incentive plans, we advocate that they should not be used to make up for a low hourly wage. A fair hourly wage, for example, should not be pegged to a labor grade. At one manufacturer, we observed a shop with three labor grades and 15 pieces of equipment. We advised the company to eliminate the labor grades and have a base wage of "x" dollars an hour. When a worker had mastered how to set up and operate five pieces of equipment, he would receive a set increase in his wage. When the operator learned five more machines, he would get another increase. When the employee learned all fifteen, he would receive the maximum rate, regardless of his seniority and the company would have a flexible worker.

AUTOMATION ISSUES

Even though we are talking about the issue of automation here, it is inextricably tied to rewards and incentives. How can a company expect its workers to respond if it is not up front about its automation plans? If you are going to reduce the work force through attrition, then tell people the truth. There should be no surprises. The company should make it clear that it believes American companies don't have to go offshore to be productive. Companies must make a strong commitment to the value of human assets. If a set-up reduction program is based on head-count reduction, it will *not* work.

UNION AND NON-UNION ENVIRONMENTS

It may surprise you to know that the last example was a union plant. Even so, there are special considerations in the union environment. We are often asked about the differences in implementing set-up reduction programs in union and non-union facilities. This is an area where many companies make mistakes, which either doom the project to failure or, at the very least, produce mediocre results.

The traditional management "mind-set" is that dealing with the union has to be "painful" and counter-productive, due to diametrically opposed objectives. Companies without unions tend to believe that any program can be implemented with ease simply because management deems it beneficial. Neither of these viewpoints could be further from the truth.

In both cases, a clear statement of objectives and a careful review of the employees' major concern ("What's in it for me?") must be made. We have found that successful and long-term results are sometimes achieved in unionized organizations because the issues are immediately put out on the table. Job security, classifications, wage rates, productivity, etc. are quickly raised by union leadership. Therefore, it is necessary to come up with workable solutions which can be addressed and finalized.

In non-union environments, these issues can be overlooked as management explains how the program is going to work to a room of people nodding their heads. What we should be aware of in these situations is that a nod of approval sometimes means "No way! Never in a million years." To combat this problem, we recommend that all companies initiate discussion of a set-up reduction program as if they were dealing with a union acting as a devil's advocate, whether or not the employees are unionized. The preparation will serve you well.

A unionized company may also want to talk with its Human Resources or Personnel Department. Explain to them that there are certain issues such as job rotation, restrictive labor grades and worker inflexibility which keep the company from being as flexible as it should be. Since flexible companies will be the competitive companies of the nineties and beyond, it is imperative that the company address these issues with the union in order to implement a set-up reduction program properly.

The best way to deal with a union is the same way you should deal with any company activity or issue—be open and frank. Talk to the union and ask for involvement. Sometimes it won't be easy because workers will remember every failed project of the past and they will look at set-up reduction as just another phase that will pass if they wait long enough. We think that unions have every right to feel that way. In the past, very few projects or implementation began with both sides sitting down and talking about what bothers them.

LABOR ISSUES

Some of the items that management and labor should talk about as they begin the implementation of a set-up reduction program have been discussed—job classifications, incentive systems, rewards, etc. There are, of course, many more issues. Below we will discuss some of the issues typically encountered.

OVERTIME

Don't assume that reducing overtime will be met with resistance. At many companies, for instance, we have found that employees are glad to stop working overtime. It gives them a chance to be with their families or to go fishing. Remember that only recently Boeing employees went on strike partly for this very reason. They didn't want to work all those extra hours. Quality of life is important.

UNION LEADERS

It must be admitted that some union members have problems with their union leaders. Sometimes, workers are more ready to accept change than the union leadership. This is a delicate area. We recommend that a company begin early to involve and educate union officials about set-up reduction, not only through classes, but with books, articles and informal conversations on the subject. It is also advisable to schedule question and answer sessions with the leadership before starting the program. Always remember to tell them that we just want them to "give set-up reduction a chance."

INFORMAL LEADERS

This is another delicate issue. The "true" leaders aren't always the appointed leaders. Management must recognize "worker-recognized" leadership, that is, informally selected leaders, the people other people look to before they act. We recommend that a company find out who these informal leaders are and include them in the same process shared with the appointed union leaders outlined above.

IMPLEMENTATION METHODS

A set-up reduction program implementation must make sense to the employees, not just to the management of a company. There must be an organized approach, based on contractual language and organizational considerations, of total involvement from the CEO to the line worker. Traditional labor and management barriers must be broken down in order for set-up reduction to succeed. One rule which must be observed at all times is to *never* violate a contractual agreement. Do only what the contract allows and nothing else.

"NOT MY JOB"

It is not uncommon to hear people in a traditional, functionally segregated environment say that it isn't their job to reduce set-up times. The issues of job classification and restriction clauses are sensitive bargaining issues. Additionally, the traditional approach to process improvements, methods, changes, etc. has centered around industrial/manufacturing engineers, not the set-up people and machine operators. Engineers were the traditional experts. Today's "World Class" definition of expert is the person who actually does the work. The only viable solution for companies is to confront these issues in the context of a long-term competitive position and company survival. Keeping our jobs *is* our job.

SHARING INFORMATION

As mentioned, open and frank communication is essential and the most productive way to implement a set-up program. There should be no hidden agendas or agencies. Trust and commitment will only come if both management and labor are well informed up front about goals, progress and problems and work together to bring that progress to reality.

JOB CLASSIFICATIONS

Companies will find that many people will become upset if they think the company is trying to reduce the complexity of their jobs in order to get rid of the highest job classification which is often reserved for set-up people. They will tell the company that it can't cut set-up time because their job classifications and wages will be reduced. Management must convince its people that they don't have to worry about wages. Employees must be convinced that the company can and will pay them more, or at least the same, if they can do changeovers more frequently and quickly. It is also essential that top management understands and believes that labor rates are only a small portion of total product cost and that their suppression is counterproductive to major cost reductions due to employee-driven set-up reduction activities.

PRODUCTIVITY VS. RATE INCREASE

Closely tied to job classifications and wages is the issue of productivity and rate increases. Some people will interpret a set-up reduction program as an attempt to increase their productivity with no increase in wages. There is a tendency to say, "Fine. If you're going to increase my productivity, then I want more dollars per hour." Essentially, this is a reasonable request and it may prove economical to increase hourly rates. Remember before that we did not advocate using incentive plans to make up for low hourly wages. Make sure, however, that any changes you make are discussed thoroughly with the bargaining unit. It probably is advisable to conduct some training and education programs about set-up reduction for the management of the union in order to show your view and foster the proper mind-set. We are not, of course, advocating that you always give pay increases. We need to stay competitive. But, you should consider sharing additional profits with those that helped bring about that productivity increase.

JOB SECURITY

Whether a company is union or non-union, job security is a major issue. The only way to handle this area is to be honest. If jobs are going to be lost, say so. If the company's survival depends on the set-up program, then say so. You will gain more support by being open. We recommend, however, that you make a commitment whenever possible to your employees that they will not lose their

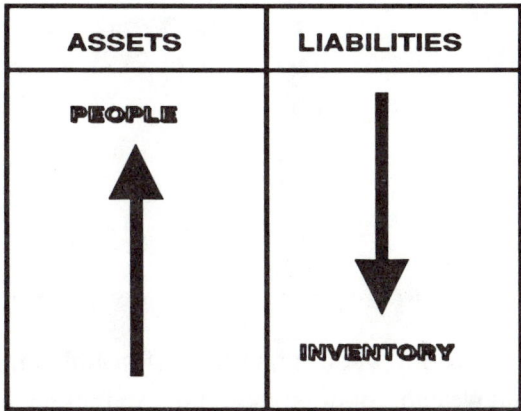

jobs. This commitment will result in a big boost in teamwork and will eliminate a major concern. People reductions should only take place as a last resort. Very few organizations are so heavily overstaffed that this is necessary. Perhaps the "T" account above of "World Class" debits and credits best describes the importance of people power. Remember that inventory on a financial statement is an asset.

LATEST BRILLIANT IDEA

We have all run into this attitude where people grow tired of
management getting on a soapbox and exhorting the latest management miracle. A few months later, when the hard work begins
and the enthusiasm lags, management discovers another miracle.
Ask almost any employee and they say the same, "All we have to
do is wait it out."

Who can blame them when management gobbles up ideas like
PacMan. What we can't understand is why so many good ideas are
discarded. Do you remember everybody being excited over Value
Analysis a few years ago and then all of a sudden nobody said a
word about it? Value Analysis is a dynamic way to reduce costs.
Why did we give up on it? When we start a program, we have to
push it and stick with it. How else will we ever know if it is
successful? All good programs are based on continuous improve-

ment. We only hurt ourselves if we discard a program when it stops producing sensational results or when its results are long-term, rather than short-term. Let's look ahead and let's get our people to look ahead. Set-up reduction is one very important part of the Continuous Improvement Process. It should not be a former brilliant idea two years from now.

MULTI-FUNCTIONAL WORKERS

This is another area to discuss with the hourly workers and upper management. Multi-functional workers will improve the competitive positions of our companies. Set-up reduction is not designed as a manpower reduction program. As we said earlier, the goal is to increase sales, not reduce employees. And, hopefully, increased sales will mean more people will need to be hired. Another point we made earlier which needs mention here is the issue of pay rates for multi-functional workers. Pay rates should be reviewed and restructured to reflect new job categories. We recommend that people be paid based on what skills they possess, not on seniority. That means they should be given the opportunity to learn new skills.

HOW TO ADDRESS LABOR FEARS

To give you an idea of how set-up programs can work, and work well, in all environments, we will relate an experience we had at a General Foods processing plant. We were conducting a training program in set-up reduction at the plant—two days of education for the program's steering committee and upper management, two days for set-up reduction team members and four hours for the remaining employees at the facility. Our goal was not to have anybody say "What is set-up reduction?" when we were finished.

In one of the employee sessions, we were about two hours or so into the presentation when we noticed that two key set-up people (one from the day shift and one from the night) were in the back of the room whispering to each other. We asked them if there was a problem.

One of them stood up and told us in no uncertain terms what he thought about the program and what we could do with it. He also told us that he was going to leave the meeting. We asked him why.

"I'm sick and tired of experts coming in," he said, "and telling us that we've been messing up all these years."

Fine, we told him. We need you to be a part of this program, but if you feel you have to leave, then go ahead. And *both* of them left.

After the session, we went to the employee's supervisor and said, "We would like to talk to this man in the conference room tomorrow at 8 a.m. for two hours."

The next morning, we got there early and set up a flip chart and put a chair in front of it. When our friend came in, we said, "Please sit down. For the next two hours, this is what we are going to do. For the first forty minutes, you will listen to us go through set-up reduction one more time. Then you will tell us your ideas about how to help the company's competitive posture."

We went through our presentation and asked him for his ideas.

"I don't have any ideas," he told us. "My only concern is that I've been doing changeovers for thirty-three years and I don't want you to make me look stupid.

We told him that we understood his feelings and then asked him if others felt the same way.

"A lot," he told us.

Thanks to this employee, we were alerted to a very important issue that we knew the company had to address before it could move forward with its implementation. The problem, in fact, centered around the issue of videotaping employees while they performed a set-up. Many of them were understandably concerned that these tapes would be used against them during job reviews. We had to assure them that this was not the purpose. (In Chapter 8, we will discuss in detail just how videotapes are used.) The consensus was that we were going to use the videotapes to make the workers look stupid, which could not be further from the truth.

The way we cleared this hurdle was to address their fears squarely. We told the set-up people that we would make a videotape of them doing a changeover. We would then give the tape to them for three weeks to watch. They could study it by themselves and make whatever improvements they wanted to the way they did the changeover. After those three weeks, we would videotape them again as they performed a changeover. When we were finished, we would give them the tape and tell them that they had to bring it to the next team meeting.

At the team meetings, the members and the set-up person would review the tape, using the changeover reduction process and look for ways to reduce set-up time. After the meeting, the set-up person could bring the tape home on the condition that he brought it back to the next meeting. When the team decided that the tape was no longer representative of the changeover (because of improvements), then a new videotape would be made and the old videotape destroyed. This was how we assured the workers that the videotapes would not be used for job reviews.

ACCEPTANCE ISSUES

One of the hardest issues a company will face in implementing a set-up reduction program is the "we vs. they" attitude. Sometimes it takes the form of one department versus another department or set-up people versus operators. Whatever form this attitude takes, it must be addressed and overcome every time it comes up. One sure way to combat this negativism is to hold team meetings on the factory floor. This not only sends a message that the factory floor is the focus of attention, but it gets the engineers and the managers to the place where they can actually see the machines which are being discussed. New insight can definitely be derived when the ivory tower with its attendant lake, fountain and ducks is abandoned for the site where *real* products are made. This technique is a variation of MBWA—Management by Walking Around.

We also need to address the issue which we call "Pride of Authorship." A company can't present an agenda of new ideas and act as though everything that has been done before is wrong. Many of the present practices were authored by the people in the factory right now. You can't come in and tell them that they are wrong and expect them to agree and gladly accept your new ideas. The employees helped build the company into what it is today. Whether their procedures are right or wrong is immaterial. They worked hard and the company has to regard their past contributions as a foundation for future growth and improvement, rather than as targets to be attacked. The way to overcome this issue is to provide education which is customized to their work environment, terminology and problems. They need to be presented with examples which they can relate to and understand.

```
┌──────────────────────────────────┐
│                                  │
│        100 % Cotton              │
│       Made in U.S.A.             │
│                                  │
│      See Reverse Side            │
│          for Care                │
│                                  │
└──────────────────────────────────┘
```

The issue of national pride is another issue of concern to many American workers. While Far Eastern techniques of set-up reduction should be fully reviewed, American applications should be emphasized. After all, many of the great strides made by the Japanese in eliminating waste are attributable to that country's reading of the works written by three Americans—Ford, Deming and Juran. Often we tell a little story to demonstrate this issue. We ask people in our training and education sessions to tell us what company we are describing and where is it located.

The company we describe takes iron ore from a mine, produces steel and then uses the steel and other material to produce a car. The whole process, from mining the iron ore to finishing an automobile, takes 81 hours. Who is that company and where is it located? Toyota? Honda? In Japan? No! That company is American. It is the Ford Motor Company of 1926. It is companies like Ford, people like Deming and Juran that the Japanese learned from. Why didn't *we* listen?

TEAMWORK

One characteristic of the Far East which helps them achieve remarkable set-up reductions is their sense of teamwork. This is certainly a lesson we can learn from. We must emphasize and reward teamwork in our companies. But, what exactly is a team? Some people confuse teams with consensus management or a slowly moving company that can't make a decision. The teams we advocate are quite the opposite. We define a team as the following:

> **TEAM (*n*) — A group of people dedicated to a common goal who have learned to build on each other's strengths and to compensate for each other's weaknesses.**

Everybody has pluses and minuses. All of us have different backgrounds and different acquired skills. Some of us are more expressive and natural leaders. Others are more analytically inclined and better at collecting and organizing data. Still others are more mechanically inclined and make excellent members of set-up reduction teams. The point is that every hand is a helping hand.

We have to get rid of what we call the "hand grenade" mentality in which one person or department thinks it's doing well and that everybody else is doing poorly. We want to break down these kind of barriers to improvement and get departments like engineering and manufacturing to work with each other about designing products which require no set-ups at all. We need to encourage set-

up people to talk with the maintenance department if there is a problem with the quality of products. We must encourage our people to begin helping each other. In reality, the "working" teams described here are better described as "hard-working" teams with a powerful orientation to getting results.

ORGANIZING FOR TEAMWORK

What the company must do in order to instill a teamwork mentality is to organize the set-up reduction process. The first step is to establish a steering committee whose job it is to manage the implementation. The set-up steering committee should consist of the following members:

- **Representatives from top management.**
- **Middle management** • **Supervisors.**
- **Hourly workers.**

We recommend a maximum of eight to ten people on this team. Larger groups become misdirected or stagnant. The team's directives are the same ones that are taught to managers in Business 101—planning, organizing, staffing, controlling and directing. During the **planning** stage, the steering committee should be discussing these questions:

- How many teams should we start out with?
- Where are they coming from?
- When are they going to meet?
- Are they going to meet on company time?

HOW MANY TEAMS AT THE BEGINNING?

We recommend beginning with four to six teams. Trying to put all of a company's employees on a team is probably too much to handle at the beginning, except in smaller companies. On the other hand, one team is too few. A question we are often asked is when to add more teams. We say that when the initial teams are functioning well, it's time to add more. Additional teams may be salted with people from the initial teams. In fact, we strongly recommend that the first teams consist of people who have good interpersonal skills, people who will eventually make good team leaders on their own team.

As for the amount of time which should be devoted to team meetings, we recommend that the time spent in a meeting be one or one and a half hours per week. We also expect each team member to spend the same amount of time outside the team meeting doing the assignments for which they volunteered. Team members should expect assignments at every team meeting. If the assignment is to collect data, the team member should organize that data for review by the team. Pareto charts, histograms, process flow charts, etc. may be required. The team member should come to the next meeting ready to share information, to brainstorm and decide what to do next, to make new assignments and then to adjourn and start working on them in preparation for the next team meeting.

So, if a team spends one and a half hours in a meeting and one and a half hours collecting data or performing their assignments, does that mean that they are working three hours a week on company time? Yes, it most definitely does. Remember that you are investing in the future of your company. If you need to ask people to work overtime to get all the work done, then that is a small price to pay, given the documented benefits of set-up reduction.

RESERVING TIME TO MEET

One more point about team meeting times: If you have two shifts, then plan the meeting at the shift change in order to include employees from both shifts. That way, each shift only loses a half hour. For example, if the shift change is at 4 p.m., then the meeting should begin at 3:30 p.m. and end at 4:30 p.m. If there are three shifts, then it will be necessary to rotate the meeting times or to have separate teams for each shift. The separate teams would work on different work centers. They would all have to abide by one rule as well. That rule would state that they have an obligation to talk to the other shift employees and pass ideas back and forth.

STEERING COMMITTEE

The steering committee must also **organize** the set-up teams so that they know what their mission is. Each team should be given a Set-Up Reduction Charter which clearly states the aims and goals of the program. The charter should not tell teams how to work on specific parts. We recommend that you let the individual set-up teams decide what is the most important problem within the guidelines set by the steering committee. The charter could simply be to reduce changeover time on Machine #2.

Another task of the steering committee is to **staff** the set-up teams. The general rule is that a team should have five to nine members and that for every salaried or management person, there should be an hourly laborer. When a team gets above nine people, there is a tendency for one or two people to do all the talking and everybody else to listen. We don't want to see this. It defeats the whole purpose of a set-up reduction team which is to have people both listen and talk. Don't be afraid to ask top management to be on a set-up team. It would be a good idea to let them and others find out what it's like to work together. Teams should also present a good cross-section of the company as well. The diagram on the next page shows one possible team configuration.

The steering committee also has the responsibility of **controlling** the set-up teams. This means that once every month the individual set-up team leaders must give a ten-minute presentation to the committee. In this report, the team leader must tell what the team has accomplished in the last month.

It is the steering committee's function to **direct** the set-up team's progress. After hearing its monthly report, the committee should decide whether the team is on track and whether they are achieving the goals of the Set-Up Reduction charter. If they aren't, then the steering committee will have to find out why and help the set-up team get back on track.

	Controller/VP Finance	Production Planning Mgr	Purchasing Manager	Quality Supervisor	Master Production Planner	Set-Up Person	Operator	Material Handler
Top Management	X							
Middle Management		X	X					
Supervisors				X				
Direct Labor					X	X	X	X

Possible Team Configuration

TEAM SELECTION

The following concerns need to be addressed in the process of team selection. First is the question of whether everyone should be involved in a set-up reduction team. We have already stated that we believe this could be unwieldy. Ideally, total involvement is the best approach but we must temper this view with reality and base team selection on the specific talent requirements needed by each team. Once the charter is established, the work of staffing can begin.

A pitfall to avoid when selecting team members is labeling a worker as "uncooperative" because he or she does not want to be on a team. For example, at one of our clients where teams were expected to meet on their time and not company time, one worker made it clear that when she was at the company, they would always get eight hours of hard work out of her. She couldn't give any more because when she went home, she had to keep the books for her husband's business. Also remember that committee meetings in an employee's personal life may preclude them from having extra time to devote to serving on a team. Our client wisely decided not to ask her to serve on the team because she was an otherwise excellent employee.

PILOT PROJECT

The next area to consider is what we call the "pilot project." A pilot project is normally undertaken to assess how the process works in your company. Therefore, you should carefully choose where to start and who will participate. Pick a good machine and assign the most cooperative, aggressive people you have. Extreme care should be taken in selecting motivated and qualified individuals in order to guarantee the success of pilot projects. We have seen some set-up programs that falter here simply because the time was not taken to pick the very best for the first few teams, the people, as we've mentioned, who will later become the core of other teams.

GETTING EMPLOYEE INVOLVEMENT

The last area to consider is whether to ask for volunteers or to hand pick team members. Volunteers, if you elect to use them, should be chosen based on the specific talents a team may need. Volunteers are often very helpful in a set-up reduction program because of the great enthusiasm they bring to the implementation. Think carefully about using volunteers, however, if you don't plan to use everybody. Nothing dampens that enthusiasm more quickly than not being used once they have been chosen. A company should consider hand-picking if there are indications that the pool of volunteers is too large and covers more than the initial scope of the program. The most difficult problem occurs when a company needs a key person, such as a set-up person, to be a team member, but this person does not volunteer. You will have to make a special effort to convince this person of his or her importance to the team. Remember: You can attract more bees with honey than vinegar.

Our recommendation is that you ask for volunteers after you have told employees the number of teams you will start with and their size. Remind everybody that if too many people volunteer, they may not be used immediately, but will be asked to serve on future teams as they are formed. If, when using this process, a key person does not volunteer, a member of the steering committee may contact that person and ask them to join the team.

MODEL SET-UP REDUCTION TEAM

What does the ideal set-up reduction team look like? First, it should include a set-up person and an operator. The remaining slots should be filled with people who possess the skills needed by the team to accomplish its objectives.

For example, if the team is on a processing line, then it may be helpful to include an industrial engineer. If the team expects to work on tool design, then, certainly, it would be wise to include a tool designer. The model set-up reduction team will include someone from the engineering disciplines.

We do advise using some caution when including engineers on a team. Engineering departments are already overburdened. To be part of still another team or project cuts deeply into its limited resources. There are two solutions. One, don't assign engineers to a team as permanent members, but make them resources to all the teams. Two, if the team is working on a problem which requires redesign, then assign a team member to the task of coordinating the interfacing with engineering. In other words, if the team wants to make a change to a tool, have somebody on the team make a sketch, bring it to engineering for review and also take it to the machine shop so that the new design can be made. In effect, this team member is relieving the engineering department of some of the "busy" work with which they may be saddled.

The model set-up team should also have a supervisor on board. This member does not necessarily have to be from the factory floor. It could be an employee from a department that supports the activity on the floor such as production planning or material control. Set-up reduction, after all, does involve cutting lot sizes, so it makes sense to have a planner on the team. The same reasoning holds true for material handlers who are in charge of bringing material to a work center and who may be preventing faster set-ups because of late delivery.

Another member may be a maintenance person, if he or she is different from the set-up person or operator. Set-up reduction teams will probably uncover numerous maintenance problems. Having a maintenance person on the team gets that coordination quickly in place. Top management should also be on the team, providing that they abide by the rule of Leader Speaks Last (LSL). Other members would perhaps come from the unions (representatives or business managers), from accounting for help in keeping measurements and statistics, from quality control if quality is a major issue or from customers (whether that is the person who buys the product or the next station on the line). Team membership ultimately should be determined by the team's needs.

TEAM LEADERSHIP

While discussing the model team, we would be remiss if we didn't talk about the qualities needed by a team leader. The leader's job is as follows:

- **Facilitate team meetings.**
- **Motivate people.**
- **Confront issues and conflicts without making people angry.**
- **Resolve differences.**
- **Watch nonverbal reactions at meetings.**
- **Prevent people from taking over meetings.**
- **Make assignments at every team meeting.**
- **Insure that assignments are being completed.**

Leaders should be free of any responsibilities during a meeting so they can focus on the above. Minutes should be taken by a designated scribe. The team leader's only assignment is a permanent one. It is his or her job to take one hour a week to be alone and to ask some searching questions:

- **How is the team doing?**
- **What do I need to do to help the team accomplish its goals?**
- **What training and education does the team need that I should provide?**

In conjunction with the responsibility of directing and supporting the team, the leader is also responsible for keeping measurement graphs and cause and effect diagrams up to date. It is his or her duty to establish where the team was when it began, where it wants to be and where it is right now on the path to its goal.

Can leaders be trained? We believe leaders need training, but that some people just won't make good leaders. Chief among those who don't make good leaders are people who believe that their way is the only way to get the job done. These people will find it difficult to embrace the philosophy of a Different Set of Eyes (DSE) in which all the different ways a job can be done are studied. The best leaders possess good interpersonal and project management skills and are well respected.

TRAINING AND EDUCATION

Both team leaders and team members will need some education and training in order to assure the success of a set-up reduction program. Outside help is often required at this point to help the team to build a solid foundation from which they can take off. Some of the areas where a team may need help in are as follows:

- **Total Business Concepts.**
- **Teambuilding techniques.**
- **Problem-solving techniques.**
- **Operator training (in order to standardize machine work).**
- **Statistical Process Control (SPC).**

FIRST LINE SUPERVISION

Set-up teams also need to establish the following policies and procedures:

- **Methods for operations.**
- **Documented set-up procedures.**
- **Operation instructions.**
- **Maintenance checklist.**

The key to the success of policies and procedure is their reinforce-
ment by supervisors. First line supervision is the cornerstone of a
set-up reduction program. They can make or break the whole
endeavor. They represent the critical link between management
and "the floor." First line supervisors must be supported and
recognized for their contributions. We need to gain their understanding of and commitment to the program so that they can
communicate its objectives with enthusiasm. They are also critical to the identification of training and education needs of the
workers. Likewise, they are critical to the establishment of baselines
and measurements. In short, supervisors are out there on the floor.
Therefore, they are best able to receive team goals and objectives,
communicate them to the floor personnel and make sure that the
team's ideas are being implemented.

Being a good supervisor may be one of the most difficult jobs in
a company. We advocate running supervisors through the following scenario to see whether or not they understand the importance
and philosophy of a set-up reduction program. We tell a supervisor that the company's best customer has just submitted a rush
order. This order will require that a certain work center must be
operated. However, the set-up person for this work center is
required to go to a team meeting. What, we ask the supervisor, do
you tell the set-up person to do? Make the part and keep the
customer happy or go to the meeting to show commitment to a
program which will make the company healthier?

The correct answer, hard as it may seem, is to do both. This may
mean working overtime. It may mean that the supervisor should
consider training another set-up person on that machine. Whatever it takes, both tasks must be accomplished. It is vitally

important not to lose sight of the fact that, in the long run, a company can't satisfy customers if team meetings are anything less than a top priority. If team meetings are postponed or all members do not consistently attend, the message is that team meetings aren't important. Once one excuse is permitted, all types of reasons for not attending meetings can be found and, before long, the teams will fall apart. Set-up reduction will come to a grinding halt and your employees will add this program to the long list of things tried in the past. Don't let the attitude of "This too shall pass." become a reality.

Attendance should not be a problem, however, once the teams get a taste of how exciting set-up reduction can be. In the next chapter, we will look at some specific methods for reducing set-up time that will generate enthusiasm in your company.

CHAPTER SEVEN

INTERNAL/EXTERNAL METHODS

When it comes to internal/external methods of set-up reduction, one of the most frequently heard acronyms is SMED, or Single Minute Exchange of Die. This method states that a company can reduce a set-up so that it can be done in the amount of time expressed by a single digit. In other words, set-ups can be reduced so that they are performed in 9 minutes or less. SMED is the creation of Shigeo Shingo, a Japanese educator and industrial engineer who developed the system as a pivotal condition of the Toyota Production System.

Mr. Shingo first came upon the idea for set-up reduction when he was asked by a manufacturing company to solve the bottleneck which was occurring at an 800-ton press. Management had decided to buy more equipment in order to eliminate the backlog, but Mr. Shingo focused instead on how long it took to change over the press. What he found out is that 47 percent of the set-up time was spent in preparation and after-adjustment, in other words, activities to get the equipment up and running at full efficiency. Another 26 percent of the time was spent on marginal operations, 24 percent on incidental operations and 3 percent on main operations. He quickly saw that simply addressing the preparation time and marginal operations could substantially reduce set-up time.

We had a client with a similar demand problem. A manufacturer of scalpels and needles, this company was running three shifts a day, seven days a week and was still unable to keep up with demand. We performed a situation analysis of the company to document precisely what was taking place. We observed set-ups and noted other areas of waste. In our assessment, we informed company management that the way to solve their demand problem was to slow the line down until it started producing all good pieces. The president of the company looked at us like we were crazy which is a fairly traditional reaction.

"Slow the line down?" he said. " How can we slow the line down? We want it to go faster. That's our problem. We can't keep up with the present demand."

The speed of production isn't your problem, we told him. Your problem is that you aren't addressing set-up time and quality problems on the line. You are producing needles so fast that they are falling on the floor and getting contaminated at final packing. You are going to have to slow down the line, study the problems and then solve them so that you can speed up the line beyond its present capacity. Once the set-up reduction team focused on the causes of set-up and quality problems, the line began producing more needles than ever before. Within three weeks, the team had eliminated scrap and increased output.

Obviously, we aren't saying that every company has to slow its line down. The point of this example is that we have to go on-site to study a problem. Without an outside examination, companies tend to focus on the wrong issues or areas. This portion of SMED provides a good beginning for the reduction of set-up time. It is not the only method. We will point out some other methods and techniques in this chapter which go beyond what is generally practiced today.

SET-UP REDUCTION:
TECHNIQUES AND ELEMENTS

Our goal, in a quick change set-up, is to have One Touch Changeover (OTC). OTC is just what it says, the continual striving for designs, equipment, tools, methods which allow a tool or die to be removed from and placed back on equipment with one motion. Some of the methodologies which are used in OTC are preset pins, auto dial-in, quarter-turn fasteners, single-thread bolts, etc. We attain OTC by looking at several elements.

INTERNAL CHANGEOVER METHODS—
The goal is to minimize the set-up steps which are done internally, or when the machine is not operating. Time spent on internal set-up steps is

unproductive downtime which should be kept to
a minimum.

EXTERNAL CHANGEOVER METHODS—
Here we want to maximize the external set-up
steps, that is, the steps which can be done while
the machine is in operation. In essence, we want
to move away from doing set-up steps while the
machine is down. Instead, we want to do more
of these steps while the machine is running.

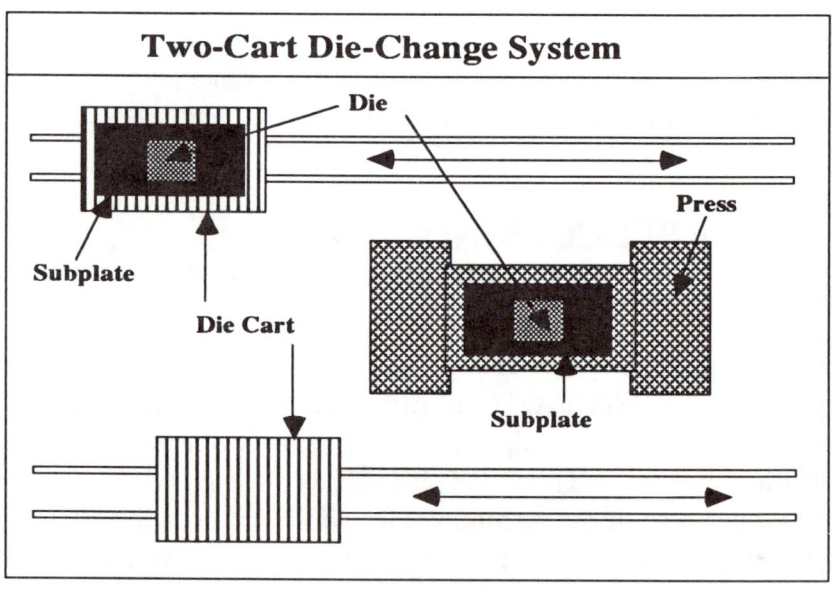

Two-Cart Die-Change System

**REMOVING AND MOUNTING APPLICA-
TIONS**—Methods should be developed and
used for simple removal and mounting of dies.
Such methods would include multiple-die sets,

pre-set tables, jigs and fixtures. Using this methodology, one of our clients was able to reduce set-up and drilling of heavy castings from one hour each to less than 10 minutes. Lot sizes and associated average inventory was reduced by 83 percent. In addition, over 3,000 hours of machining capacity was generated, thus, alleviating a major bottleneck.

ADJUST AND TRIAL PROCESS—This is an area in which companies need to develop techniques to minimize the amount of time spent in this part of a set-up. Some methods are preset positioning, stops, limit switches, automatic gauging, etc. The team should strive to achieve a positive, repeatable position in which no adjustments are required and the first piece is always a good one.

All of these techniques are used to reduce the time involved in the two basic elements of all set-ups—**internal set-up** and **external set-up**. Internal set-up, those elements which must be carried out while the machine is shut down, needs to address the removal and attachment of dies, fixtures, tools and gauges. External set-up are those elements which can take place while the machine is in operation. An example of this is returning parts to storage or transporting new parts to the machine, getting and checking all hand and power tools, nuts, bolts, gauging, etc. ahead of time and insuring that everything is in a good state of repair.

Given these definitions and the techniques above, our strategy for reducing set-up time is simply the separation of internal and external elements, the shifting of internal set-up elements to external set-up and then the reduction of both internal and external elements. A word of caution here: Simply separating or shifting to external is not enough. A team must not stop until internal and external changeover time is reduced substantially. A 50 to 75 percent reduction should be the bare acceptable minimum.

PROCEDURES AND OPERATIONS

Whatever the process, product or equipment used, all set-ups break down into five categories.

SET-UP CATEGORIES	
1	**Organization Checks**
2	**Installation and Removal**
3	**Locating and Setting the Tools**
4	**Adjustment of Settings**
5	**Final Adjustments**

The first category is **Organization Checks**. These are the steps taken by a set-up person to insure that all the needed material, tools, dies, fixtures, etc. are:

- **Available.**
- **Defect-free.**
- **Working correctly.**
- **Maintained properly.**

It seems obvious that you should have the right tools and material on hand, but it is unfortunately not always the case in manufacturing companies. We routinely observe operators, using tools which are worn out, trying to make products which have to meet tolerances to the thousandths of an inch. These tools need to be replaced. Is management failing to provide sufficient and necessary resources? Does the operator practice preventive maintenance?

This area can present a substantial "mind-set" hurdle to be overcome. In most cases, people want to a good job and help their company save money. Traditionally, this may have meant getting by with whatever tools were available. This practice, unfortunately, reminds us of the old adage: "Penny wise and pound foolish."

The second category is **Installation and Removal**. This is truly the business of set-up—taking an old job off a machine and putting a new job on. Ideally, a company should get set-ups down to just this step. It should certainly account for the majority of the time in a set-up.

The third category of set-up activity is **Locating and Setting the Tools**. This is where we put the tools into the work center. It is not the precise setting that comes later, but it does get close.

The fourth category is **Adjustment of Settings**. Examples of this category are getting temperatures right when making glass products, adjusting dimensions for drilling, cutting or bending, setting pressure, proper filling of bottles or packages, etc.

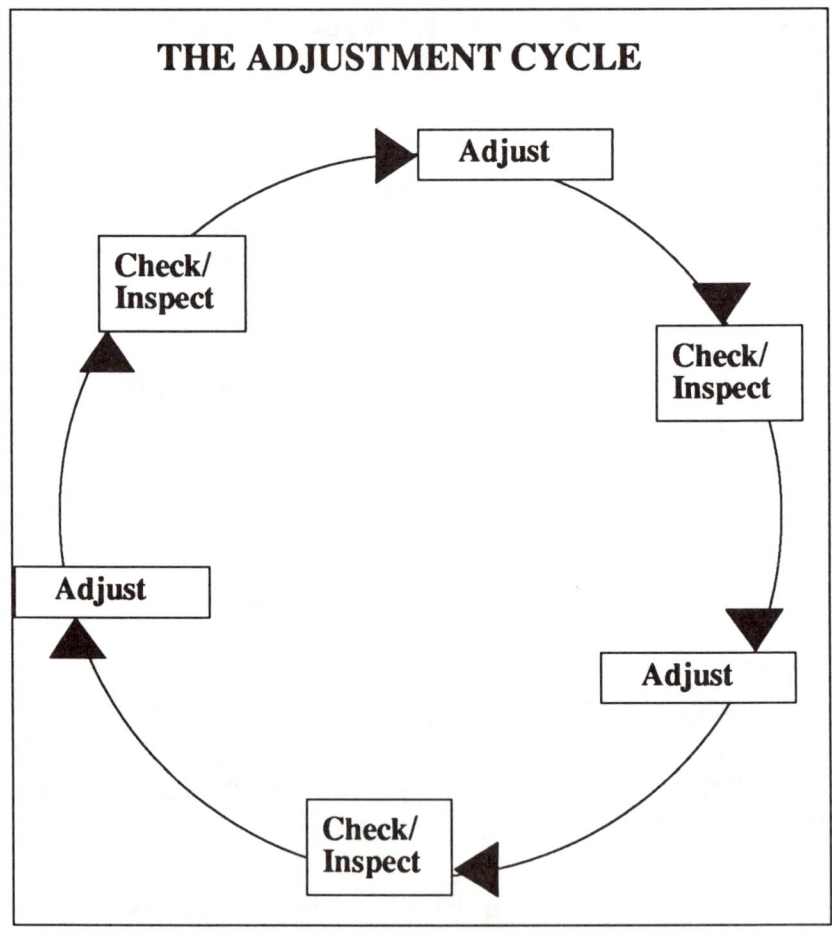

THE ADJUSTMENT CYCLE

Adjust

Check/ Inspect

Check/ Inspect

Adjust

Adjust

Check/ Inspect

The fifth category, **Final Adjustments**, is the verification of the previous categories. It is all the activities used by a set-up person or operator to adjust and try a part until the equipment is running at full efficiency. Some of these activities are making sure the tooling is on center or making sure settings are correct.

If you were to observe a typical set-up and then break the activities down into the five categories above, the percentage of time spent in each category would approximate these figures:

CATEGORY	PERCENTAGE
1. Organization Checks.	20%
2. Installation and Removal	5%
3. Locating and Setting the Tools	10%
4. Adjustment of Settings	15%
5. Final Adjustments	50%
Total	100%

This chart makes it very obvious as to where a company should concentrate its set-up reduction efforts. We are often asked whether it is a good idea in set-up reduction to add 5 minutes to category two or three in order to eliminate 20 minutes in category five. Yes, it is a very good idea. But, once that is done, then we encourage them to start working on eliminating the 5 added minutes. Above all else, set-up reduction is a *continuous improvement process*.

SET-UP REDUCTION STAGES

In most companies, it is helpful to begin set-up reduction by addressing the internal and external pieces of the set-up. The preliminary observation of the set-up will show that the internal and external components are not differentiated. The first stage, then, is to separate these two components so that it is clear which operations can be done when the equipment is running and which operations presently can be done only when the equipment is not running.

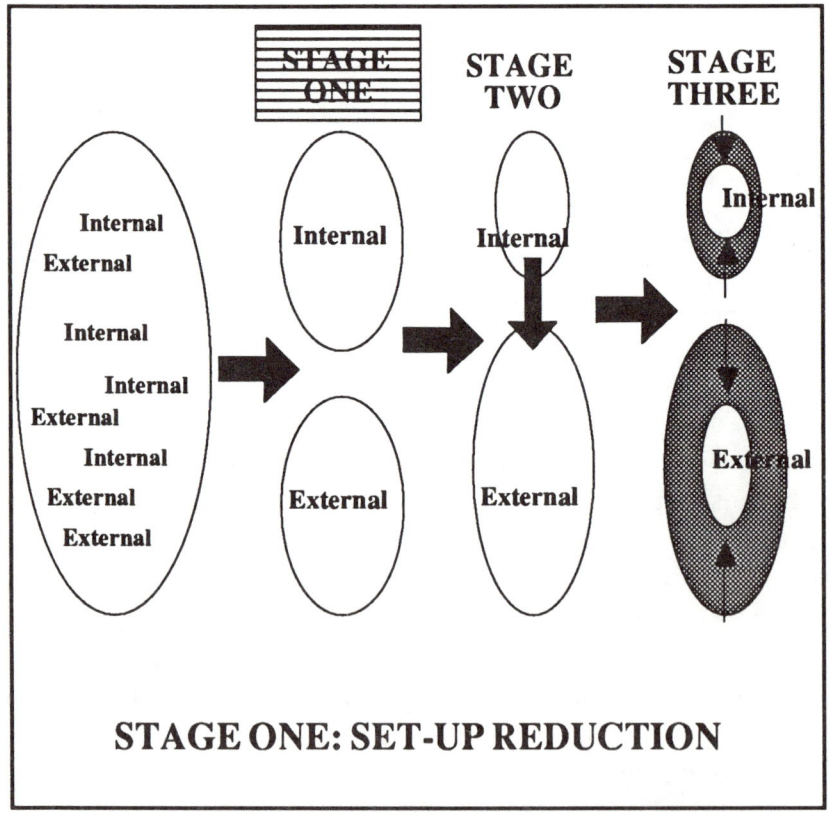

STAGE ONE: SET-UP REDUCTION

The next stage is to see if it is possible to shift any of the internal components to external components. For example, we found at Cosmair, the U.S. manufacturing arm of L'Oréal Cosmetics, that it was effective to buy duplicate valves and feed lines for one of their lotion filling lines. Then, when a line was switched over, it was possible to attach the duplicate valves and lines which were already clean to the equipment and to clean out the first set externally while the equipment was running. Previously, the cleaning step was done internal to the set-up, that is, when the equipment was not running. Now it is done while the equipment is producing.

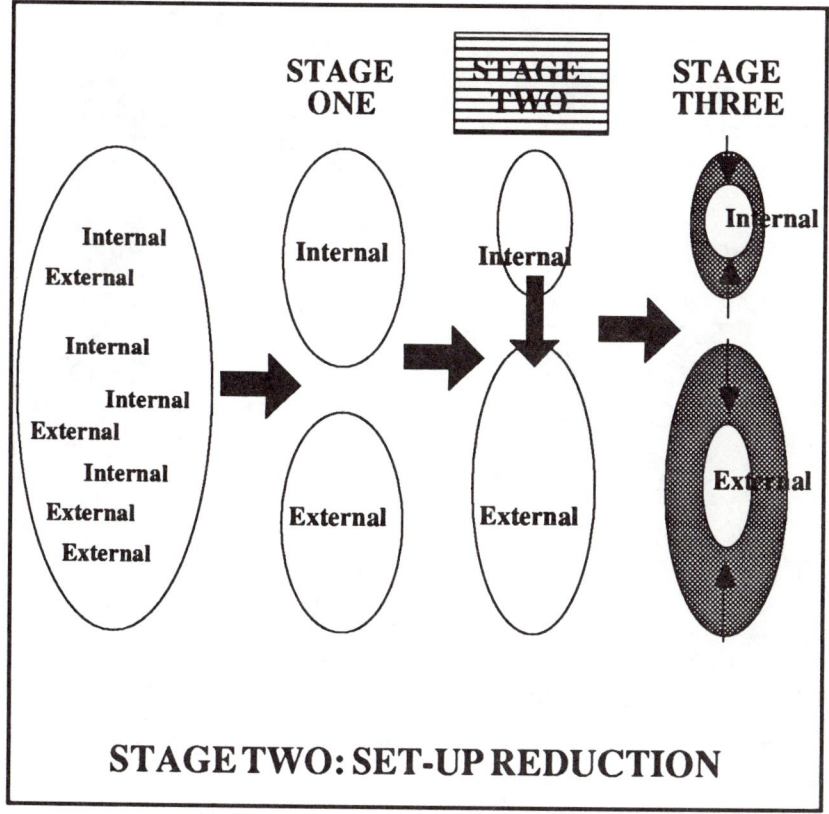

STAGE TWO: SET-UP REDUCTION

The third stage is to take the newly formulated external and internal categories and reduce their elements.

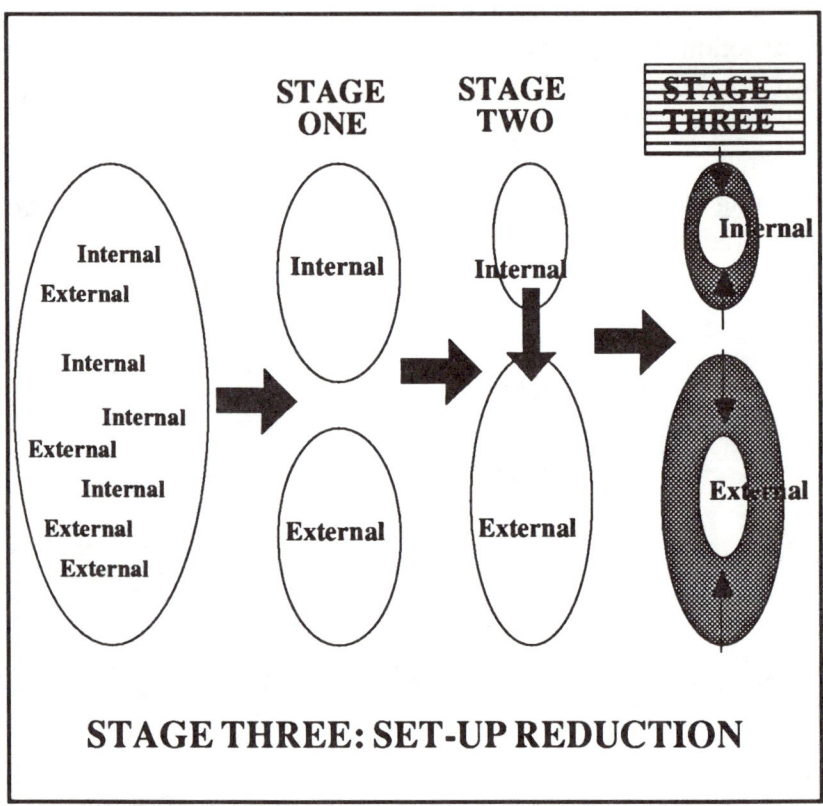

STAGE THREE: SET-UP REDUCTION

SEPARATE INTERNAL FROM EXTERNAL

In the first stage during which a company separates the internal and external components of the set-up, it is recommended that you develop checklists, perform function checks and change how tools and dies are transported.

CHECKLISTS

Checklists overcome mistakes. A checklist should include everything which is necessary to the operation, such as:

— Specifications required.

— Names of qualified workers.

— Tooling required.

— Operating conditions—what are the most efficient/optimal settings and operating conditions? You should determine these conditions when the line is running at peak efficiency and then start setting up for these same conditions.

— Measurements required to insure set-ups are performed properly. Let us make a special note here. When it comes to determining the very best settings, there is no better time to obtain those settings than when the line or equipment is running well. We have observed, however, that most companies do not attempt to determine why or when he equipment is running well. We recommend that you document speeds, feeds, temperature settings, etc. Then, when the line is not running well, you may find that using these documented settings eliminates the problem. The next step would be to accomplish these settings during the changeover and thus make it a perfect quick change.

FUNCTION CHECKS

Immediately after an operation, workers should follow a function check flowchart which would include the following:

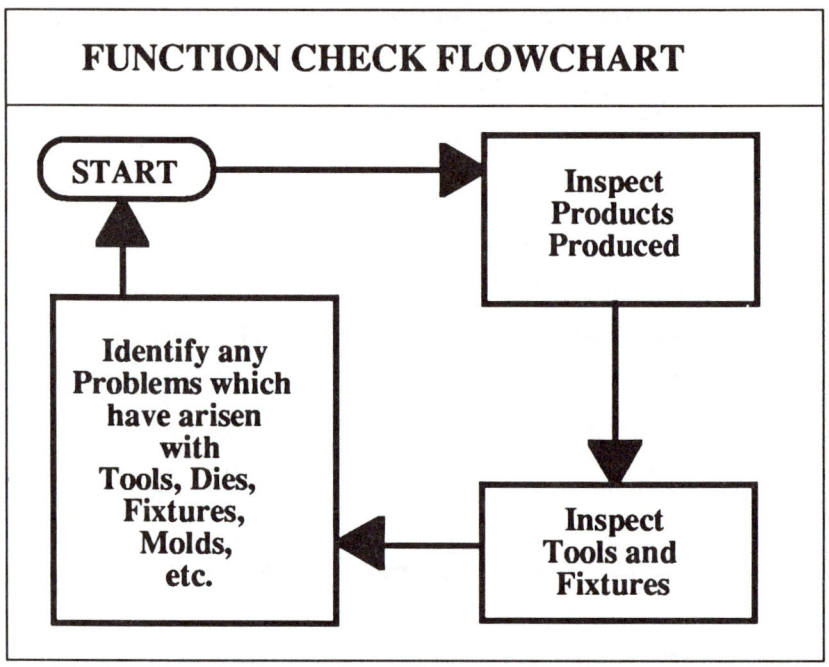

FUNCTION CHECK FLOWCHART

START → Inspect Products Produced → Inspect Tools and Fixtures → Identify any Problems which have arisen with Tools, Dies, Fixtures, Molds, etc. → START

The goal is that no repairs should be required during the next changeover. Often, while accomplishing a set-up, a problem is found with a tool which should have been identified the last time the job was run. Typically, however, the tool is taken off the work center and put into storage. Nothing was done to correct the problem. Whose responsibility is it to see that all the tools and dies necessary to an operation are in a good state of repair and ready to run? The last person who put the tool or die on the shelf. If the operator knows a problem exists with the tool, he should communicate that information to the set-up person.

If someone knows a tool or die is not performing correctly, it is that person's responsibility to write a maintenance work order. By the way, maintenance work orders that say "This tool won't work", won't work. When a person writes this sentence or writes "Defective" or "Won't run," that tells us nothing. If a worker can't explain what is wrong, then he or she should show a sample part to Maintenance and mark the error or defect.

What is Maintenance's job? To fix the tool or die *immediately*. We don't want them to call up Production Scheduling and ask when the tool is going to be run next so that they can get around to fixing it just before that time. The next planned run may be four weeks away, but the customer could call tomorrow and ask for a rush order. What is going to happen if that defective die has been sitting on the shelf waiting to be repaired? Somebody is going to take it down and use it anyway. And the result will be the production of more defective parts.

TRANSPORTING DIES

Changing how we transport dies and tools is the third technique for separating internal and external set-up operations. Basically, this means that, during external set-up, we should:

- Transport tools, dies, jigs, gauges, etc. from storage areas to machines.

- Transport old dies from machines to die storage areas, toolrooms or maintenance.

Many companies say that they can't improve the transporting of tools or dies. One company said that they couldn't make any improvements in transportation because they had to keep their tools in a cleaning room. We asked why they couldn't move the room closer to the work center. There was no reason they couldn't. At another company, a similar situation arose. This company decided not to move their cleaning room, but they outfitted their transportation system so that it could keep tools and dies clean as they were moved around the factory floor and as they sat at work centers waiting for the next job. Where there's a will, there's a way.

MOVING INTERNAL TO EXTERNAL

At this point an attempt is made to shift the internal components of a set-up to the external side so that these can be done while the equipment is still running. First, the set-up reduction team should look at the function and purposes of each operation in the internal set-up. Then, when we have found activities for the shift, the team should decide the best way to move the internal component to the external side. This is a good time to take a second look at the set-up. As the observation is made, look for the following areas:

- What advance preparation of operating conditions—preheating jigs, for example—could be done externally?

- Color-coding of required tools, dies and fixtures to make them easy to identify and control, e.g., the red tooling goes with the red machine.

- Function standardization—could we standardize the shape of tools and dies so they can run more than one type of job? Or, standardize so that the holding fixtures do not have to be changed or adjusted?

- Use of intermediary jigs—standardize where you lift different tools so that the lifting devices do not require adjustment and use intermediary jigs to set the job up externally.

REDUCING INTERNAL AND EXTERNAL TIME

This stage takes the categories of both internal and external set-up operations and shrinks the time needed for each to a minimum. External operations are shrunk by making still more improvements in the storage and transport of tools, dies, jigs, gauges, etc. This requires an organized tool room in which the tools are maintained on a regular schedule and kept in the required quantities. It may also require special transport equipment such as roller tables, air transfer tables, etc.

Internal operations are improved by using one or more of the following five techniques:

- **Simultaneous activities**—If possible, use two people for a set-up to eliminate one set-up person going from one side of the equipment to another. In simultaneous operations, we need to determine what steps in the set-up could be done at the same time.

- **Improving clamping methods**—Threads, bolts and fasteners slow down changeovers. Are you torquing because you need to or because it's nice to get them tight? Consider using one-turn methods such as the pear-shaped hole, U-slots, clamps, U-shaped washers or the split-thread method. Or one-motion methods such as cam clamps, spring stops, taper pins, wedges, magnets and vacuum suction. Or interlocking methods where two parts are locked together like pieces of a puzzle.

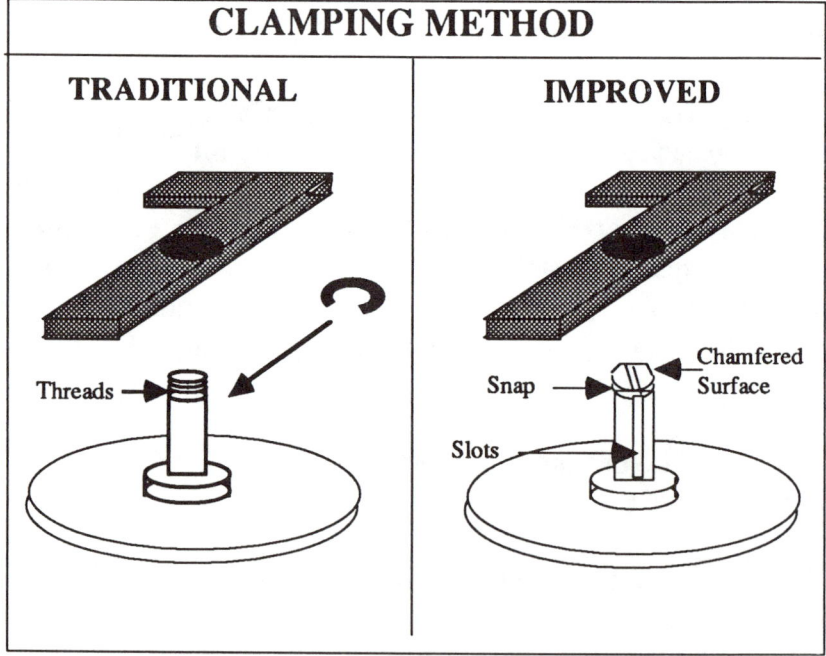

CLAMPING METHOD

TRADITIONAL	IMPROVED

Threads

Snap — Chamfered Surface

Slots

- **Precision adjustments**—The repeated adjustments typical of most set-ups as they are readied for processing are the result of imprecise settings made during locating and setting adjustments. One way to solve this problem is to use constant numerical values. For example, use only a graduated center line to eliminate adjustments which "sneak up" on a setting. Operators may already use magic markers to highlight the spots they adjust to, so why not just standardize the practice? Another way to eliminate adjustments is to use v-blocks on a machine or a table in order to precisely center tools, dies or parts in one motion.

• **Least Common Multiple (LCM) System—** The basic principle of LCM, which was developed by Mr. Shingo, is to leave the mechanism alone and change only the function. For instance, the goal is to make settings, not adjustments. Instead of using one limit switch which must first be adjusted to mark off the correct length of wiring or tubing before actually cutting the length and finally loosening, adjusting, tightening and making the next part and so on until the cut is correct, LCM says to use several preset limit switches so that all the adjustments can be made by activating the limit switch for the required setting.

• **Automation**—The main issue to remember about automation is that other set-up reduction techniques reduce changeover time by much more and they cost much less. For example, we find that it is possible to reduce set-up time up to 80 or 90 percent simply by using reduction techniques. By automating, you may be able to get set-ups down to less than 5 percent of the original time. The point is that automation is the last step. Many companies have tried to automate first and have wasted money and time. The areas to consider for automation after you have used other set-up reduction techniques are:

- Tool movement—to and from the machine.
- Die clamping.
- Electric drives for adjustments.
- Presetting of operating conditions.
- Feeding of material.

The key to automation is judicious application. You may think automation will be a springboard for set-up reduction in your company. It is not the place to begin when looking for solutions or a framework for finding ways to improve. Automation is the last step in set-up reduction. Companies should first consider the internal/external method. There are other methods. In the next chapter, we will take a look at another proven method that will advance a company toward quick change.

CHAPTER EIGHT

VIDEOTAPE METHOD

We firmly believe that making videotapes of set-ups is the most effective way to record and analyze a changeover's components in order to reduce the overall set-up time. Before you buy or rent a video camera and charge down to your factory floor, there are some guidelines to follow so that the maximum benefit can be obtained. Even before someone in the company begins taping, there should be a Pre-Videotape Checklist which the camera operators should go through before taping. Nothing is more frustrating than to arrange to tape a set-up and find out that the machine doesn't work or that the operator doesn't know how to operate the camera. In addition, to proper working condition and

knowledge of operation, the camera operator should have sufficient expertise to fix problems which occur frequently, such as
batteries wearing out. The operator should also read the instructions and practice using the equipment before taping a set-up.

Any answers of "no" to the Pre-Videotape Checklist on the next
page should be addressed and solved before videotaping begins.
Once the pre-videotape step is completed, the camera operator
must now make sure that a complete record of the set-up is taped.
The tape should begin before the last part of the previous run is
completed. As soon as that part is completed, the camera operator
should immediately begin the clock. The video itself should
include:

- **Preparing the set-up — obtaining tools,
  materials, etc.**
- **Tearing down the old job.**
- **Putting on the new job.**
- **Getting the job to run right.**
- **Inspecting first pieces.**
- **Searching for missing tools, etc.**
- **Replacing broken tools, etc.**
- **Finding solutions to any problems.**

The camera operator must also make sure that all movements of
the set-up person are visible. This means getting the "choreogra-
phy" of the set-up, rather than detailed hand movements. Closeups should only be used if the movements are critical to understanding the set-up. In general, closeups are not necessary. The
set-up person will be able to tell the team what the person was
doing when the videotape is reviewed.

PRE-VIDEOTAPE CHECKLIST

	Yes	No

Set Up and Operate Camera and Recorder

    1. Cables, plugs, etc. attached?   ___ ___

    2. Does clock attachment work?   ___ ___

    3. Camera attached to tripod?   ___ ___

    4. Are all controls operational?   ___ ___

Lighting Check

    1. Is lighting adequate for taping?   ___ ___

    2. Are extra lights operational?   ___ ___

    3. Are extension cords available?   ___ ___

Camera Location

    1. Can I see the overall process?   ___ ___

    2. Is camera location disruptive to
       the overall environment?   ___ ___

Power Source

    1. Is there an AC power source nearby?   ___ ___

    2. Will I need more cable, cords, etc.?   ___ ___

    3. Batteries tested/charged?   ___ ___

    4. Do I need extra batteries?   ___ ___

Miscellaneous

    1. Has set-up person been notified
       in advance?   ___ ___

    2. Have nearby operators been notified?   ___ ___

Equipment

    1. Missing equipment?   ___ ___

It is also a good idea to make the set-up person feel as comfortable as possible. We often suggest doing practice videotapes so that nobody gets "stage fright." Furthermore, it is absolutely vital that the videotape be an accurate picture of an average set-up and not of a perfect set-up. Set-up people should not rehearse for their "role" in the tape. When the set-up reduction team analyzes the videotape, it is absolutely essential that they see all the problems and delays which are normally encountered. In fact, it would be wise to ask the set-up person whether all typically occurring problems appear on the videotape.

The checklist below is suggested as a means to check the quality of the actual taping and to check the content of the tape:

VIDEOTAPE CHECKLIST

	Yes	No
Did videotape show last piece of previous run?	___	___
Were all set-up people always visible?	___	___
Were beginning and end of each element visible?	___	___
Camera in right position to see all elements?	___	___
Was the lighting adequate?	___	___
Was the clock readable?	___	___
Did videotape show when first piece made?	___	___
Did videotape continue until first good piece?	___	___
Did videotape continue until planned production rate was achieved?	___	___

Once the videotape has been completed, it must be documented by the set-up person and by the leader of the set-up reduction team so that the team can analyze the different elements, or activities. The Videotape Analysis Form below divides the videotaped set-up into "bite-size" pieces which can be observed by the team as a preliminary to the problem-solving techniques described earlier. It's impossible to make any lasting improvements unless there is a documented record of the current set-up. This is the reason why we videotape and document the set-up on Analysis Forms as shown in Figure 1 below.

SET-UP REDUCTION
VIDEOTAPE ANALYSIS

Current Method								Proposed Method	
Non-Value Added Activity	Value Added Activity	Seg-ment Number	Segment Description / ElementDescription	A C	Current Time	I C	Pro-posed Time	Non-Value Added Activity	Value Added Activity
			Totals						

Filling in the Analysis Form is relatively easy. How long it requires depends upon the length of time it takes to perform the set-up and its complexity. Whatever the degree of difficulty, there are three steps:

> **Step One:**   **Identify and time elements.**
> **Step Two:**   **Code elements.**
> **Step Three:** **Evaluate all the set-up elements.**

STEP ONE: The first step helps the set-up team find out where the most time is being spent and, thus, where the most time reduction can be obtained. In addition, the first step allows the team to measure how much each segment is reduced from videotape to videotape.

In Figure 2 on the following page, the set-up person and team leader have begun to fill out the form. After reviewing the videotape, they see that the first segment of the set-up is devoted to replacing the vacuum manifold. The team leader puts a "1" in the Segment Number column and writes "Replace vacuum manifold" in the Segment Description column. The example below also lists a few of the elements which compose this particular segment of the set-up.

Now the team leader and set-up person review the tape again to see how much time was taken for each of the elements. If you are not able to get a video camera with a clock attachment which shows the running time in the frame, it is possible to time the elements using a stop watch. Click it on when the element begins and click it off when the element ends. Whatever method you use to time the set-up elements, you will record the times under the heading,

Figure 2

SET-UP REDUCTION
VIDEOTAPE ANALYSIS

Current Method							Proposed Method		
Non-Value Added Activity	Value Added Activity	Seg-ment Number	Segment Description / Element Description	A C	Current Time	I C	Pro-posed Time	Non-Value Added Activity	Value Added Activity
		1	*Replace vacuum manifold*		*∅*				
			- disconnect vacuum line		*:43*				
			- get tools		*2:02*				
			- remove 2 nuts		*3:23*				
			- remove old manifold		*3:37*				
			- replace new manifold		*4:06*				
			- replace 2 nuts		*5:27*				
			- connect vacuum line		*6:30*				
			Totals						

AC (Activity Code)
1. Preparation
2. Remove/Replace
3. Align/Adjust
4. Test/Verify
5. Interruption

IC (Improvement Code)
A. Checklist
B. Maintenance
C. Equipment change
D. Tool change
E. Procedure change

Current Method, on the left side of the form. You will notice two columns under this heading—Non-Value Added Activity and Value Added Activity. If the element under consideration was "non-value added," put the recorded time in that column. If the element was "value-added," put the recorded time in the appropriately named column.

In Figure 3 on the following page, "disconnecting the vacuum line" was determined to be a value-added activity. Therefore, the ":43" (the amount of time spent on this element) was placed in the "value-added" activity column. "Getting tools," however, was judged to be a non-value added activity. Therefore, the time spent on this element was placed in the "non-value added" activity column. Meanwhile, a running total of the time is kept in the column headed "Current Time." The form on the next page shows what the set-up person and team leader have done to this point.

STEP TWO: The reason for the second step is to aid the set-up reduction team in identifying the groups of activities, or elements, which take the most amount of time. For example, the most time consuming activity at one work center may be preparation. This would show up in the A/C column. There would be a substantial number of "1's" in this column with respect to the other codes.

In Figure 4 on Page 186, the team leader and set-up person have used the accompanying activity code to identify all the elements. As can be seen, a majority of the activities were in the "Remove/ Replace" category. It came as no surprise then that as the new set-up developed, most of the improvements came in this "activity" category.

Figure 3

SET-UP REDUCTION
VIDEOTAPE ANALYSIS

Non-Value Added Activity	Value Added Activity	Seg-ment Number	Segment Description / Element Description	A C	Current Time	I C	Pro-posed Time	Non-Value Added Activity	Value Added Activity
			Current Method				**Proposed Method**		
1:19	:43	1	Replace vacuum manifold		∅				
			– disconnect vacuum line		:43				
	1:21		– get tools		2:02				
	:14		– remove 2 nuts		3:23				
			– remove old manifold		3:37				
	:29		– replace new manifold		4:06				
	1:21		– replace 2 nuts		5:27				
	1:03		– connect vacuum line		6:30				
			Totals						

AC (Activity Code)
1. Preparation
2. Remove/Replace
3. Align/Adjust
4. Test/Verify
5. Interruption

IC (Improvement Code)
A. Checklist
B. Maintenance
C. Equipment change
D. Tool change
E. Procedure change

Figure 4

SET-UP REDUCTION
VIDEOTAPE ANALYSIS

Current Method							Proposed Method		
Non-Value Added Activity	Value Added Activity	Seg-ment Number	Segment Description / Element Description	A C	Current Time	I C	Pro-posed Time	Non-Value Added Activity	Value Added Activity
		1	Replace vacuum manifold		∅				
	:43		−disconnect vacuum line	2	:43				
1:19			− get tools	5	2:02				
	1:21		− remove 2nuts	2	3:23				
	:14		− remove old manifold	2	3:37				
	:29		− replace new manifold	2	4:06				
	1:21		− replace 2nuts	2	5:27				
	1:03		− connect vacuum line	2	6:30				
			Totals						

AC (Activity Code)

1. Preparation
2. Remove/Replace
3. Align/Adjust
4. Test/Verify
5. Interruption

IC (Improvement Code)

A. Checklist
B. Maintenance
C. Equipment change
D. Tool change
E. Procedure change

STEP THREE: The third step makes it clear where to begin problem-solving, where to use fishbone diagrams and where to employ internal/external methods of set-up reduction. In essence, it sets the stage for the implementation of various projects or plans which will result in a greatly reduced set-up time. The team leader takes the Analysis Form which is completely filled out, except for the last few columns under the heading of "Proposed Method." These columns are filled by the team and the set-up person as they review each element. The team's job is to develop possible solutions based on previously learned problem-solving techniques and internal/external set-up reduction methods and then to implement the best ideas. The intent, of course, is to find a new method for completing an element of the set-up which only adds value to the activity. Ideally, all non-value added activities should be completely eliminated.

In Figure 5 on the next page, you will see that the team leader has filled in the last two columns on the right, based on whether the proposed method is value-added or non-value added. It is important to note that the goal is continuous improvement and not to study the problem to death. Realistically, a team will not eliminate all non-value added items on the first pass. Cut the set-up time in half and then go back and continue the process until quick change is achieved.

At the same time, the team has estimated how long the proposed method will take and noted that in the column headed by "Proposed Time." The first column in the "Proposed Method" section contains a letter which corresponds to the Improvement Code listed below.

Figure 5

SET-UP REDUCTION
VIDEOTAPE ANALYSIS

Current Method							Proposed Method		
Non-Value Added Activity	Value Added Activity	Seg-ment Number	Segment Description / Element Description	A C	Current Time	I C	Pro-posed Time	Non-Value Added Activity	Value Added Activity
		1	Replace vacuum manifold		∅				
	:43		– disconnect vacuum line	2	:43	C	∅		
1:19			– get tools	5	2:02	C	∅		
	1:21		– remove 2 nuts	2	3:23	C	∅		
	:14		– remove old manifold	2	3:37	C	∅		
	:29		– replace new manifold	2	4:06	C	∅		
	1:21		– replace nuts	2	5:27	C	∅		
	1:03		– connect vacuum line	2	6:30	C	∅		
	Solution:		made adjustable manifold	→		C	:43		:43
1:19	**5:11**		Totals		**6:30**		**:43**	**∅**	**:43**

AC (Activity Code)
1. Preparation
2. Remove/Replace
3. Align/Adjust
4. Test/Verify
5. Interruption

IC (Improvement Code)
A. Checklist
B. Maintenance
C. Equipment change
D. Tool change
E. Procedure change

Once the Videotape Analysis Form has been completed, it provides the team with a "snapshot" of what the set-up looked like originally and how it is being reduced. In one glance, top management or other teams in the plant can see what the team has done and plans to do. The form is both a documentation of progress and a model for future progress by other teams, plants or divisions.

IMPLEMENTATION PROCESS

The next step brings us to the implementation process. One way to determine where to begin reducing set-up time is to make a list of all the elements of the set-up which begins with the activity taking the longest amount of time and so on down to the activity which takes the least amount of time. Again, this helps the team identify where the most significant time savings can be obtained. Set-up reduction typically goes through a five-step implementation process.

STEP ONE: ESTABLISH STEERING COMMITTEE

In the first step, the company *establishes a steering committee*. Work centers, or areas of opportunity, are selected to be the focus of the set-up reduction program. The steering committee now selects set-up reduction teams. Goals and charters are then set for each team to achieve.

STEP TWO: INVOLVE THE WORKFORCE

The second step, which in reality is concurrent with the first step, is to *involve the workforce*. This is accomplished by meeting with the staff, set-up teams, targeted departments, manufacturing supervisors and other employees. In fact, we recommend that the whole company get some education in set-up reduction, at least a two-hour workshop, so that different departments can talk the same language with each other. Education encourages cross-fertilization of ideas and that is always the key criteria for success. While educating your company, be prepared to give your people the following:

- **A clear understanding of set-up reduction.**
- **A positive climate to attack problems.**
- **An environment for active participation.**

STEP THREE: DOCUMENT THE SET-UP

In the third step, the set-up reduction team should be actively *documenting the set-up*. This would primarily be the creation of a videotape of the set-up and the completion of an Analysis Form as described above.

STEP FOUR: IMPROVE THE SET-UP

This sets the stage for the fourth step, *improving the set-up*, in which the set-up team uses fishbone diagrams, preventive maintenance guidelines and problem-solving techniques to find solutions. Then the team works together to prepare for the implementation of set-up reduction.

STEP FIVE: ACHIEVE QUICK CHANGE

The fifth step, *achieving quick change*, may seem obvious, but all too often we see companies develop solutions and then think they have solved the problem just because they found out how. Problems don't get solved unless people use their brainpower to find a solution and then use their perseverance to put the plan into action. The best way to make sure that a set-up team's solutions get put into action is to establish a system for measuring the improvement in performance. In other words, document that the solution has been put into place and then track its progress. If there is no documentation, then you know that the solution has probably not been implemented.

In the next chapter, we will look at a number of applications of set-up reduction methods. All of the applications have used the problem-solving techniques, the internal/external methods and the videotape methods previously explained. Together, these three methods and techniques are a powerful weapon in the war against waste in our companies. You will see that the methods of set-up are indeed powerful enough and flexible enough to be applied to a number of different situations. Set-up reduction is not restricted to the factory floor.

CHAPTER NINE

APPLICATIONS

The applications covered in this chapter are a compilation of actual set-up experiences at clients and companies in North America. Our advice is not to search only for applications which are taken from a specific industry. Very often, we find that people learn from examples which, at first glance, seem to have little to do with their own industries. In other words, job shops can learn set-up applications from repetitive industry; repetitive manufacturers from the process industry; and process manufacturers from job shops.

The applications of set-up are like the applications of any discipline. Certain basic laws apply in any kind of industry or at any type of manufacturer. Therefore, when you read the following applications, search and note the *principle* behind the actual technical steps. This principle will, in many cases, have a direct application at your company.

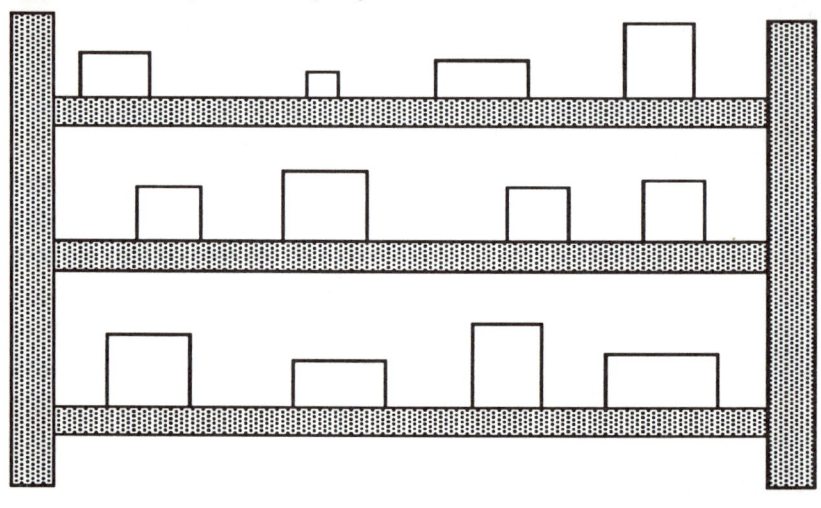

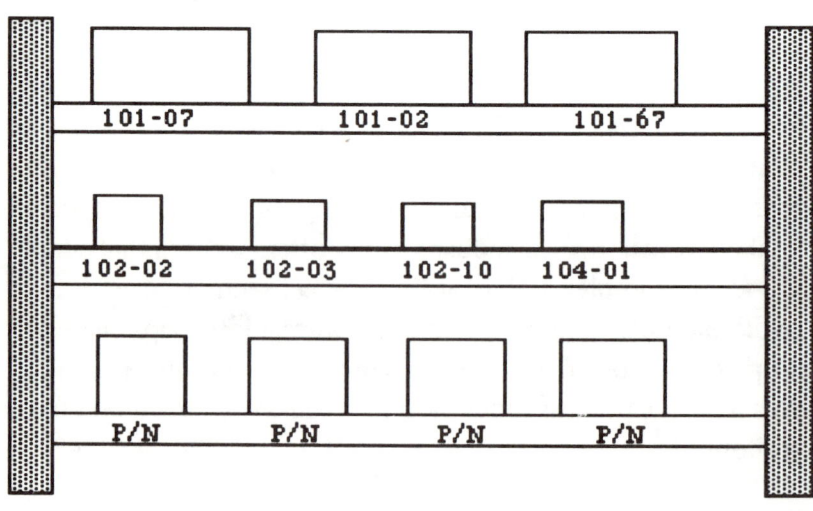

TOOL AND DIE STORAGE

As noted earlier, locating tools and dies often uses up inordinate amounts of time in the performance of a set-up. We stopped counting the number of times we have observed set-up people walking back and forth to tool rooms in their search for a fifty-cent hex wrench. And we stopped being amazed at the number of unorganized, cluttered tool rooms we have encountered where set-up people spend valuable time trying, often in vain, to find a drill or tap. This practice is completely unnecessary. There is one thing that can be done now — organize tool and die storage areas and to locate them as close as possible to the work center as shown on the previous page.

Proximity to Use: Whenever possible, tools and dies should be stored at or near the point of production use. Segregation by work

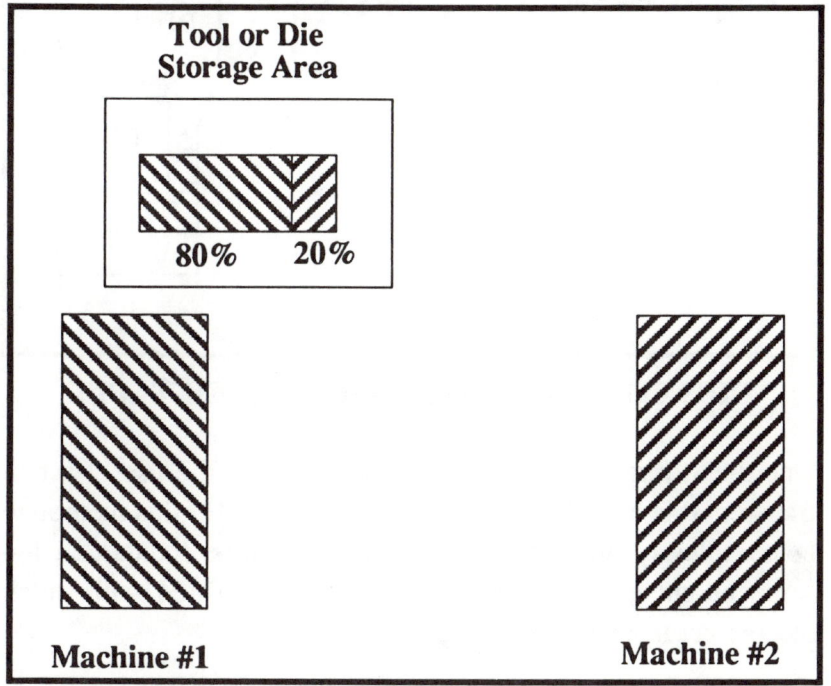

center cell, product line, etc. are possible location schemes. If many pieces of equipment in a plant require the use of a tool or die, locate the tool next to the piece of equipment which uses it 80 percent of the time. Come and get the tool or die the remaining 20 percent of the time.

Organization: Tools and dies should be clearly marked and assigned to a specific location (not simply a general shop area). All tools and dies should always be returned to this location after use, in "production-ready" condition, meaning that all maintenance, repairs and function checks should have been completed.

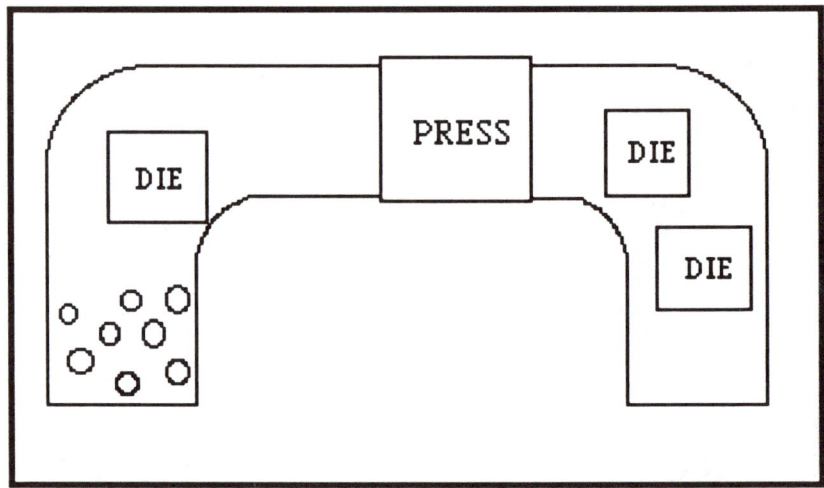

DIES LOCATED ON BALL TRANSFER TABLE

One die storage method which works well is the use of a ball transfer table at the machine location. In order for this method to be completely successful, all the dies should be standardized—same height and base size—and should be fitted with quick disconnect fasteners or fittings.

TOOL RACK

One of the best analogies for organizing tools came from a worker at a client. On weekends, this employee was a member of the pit crew at local speedway. His job, as he told us, was to replace the left rear tire when his driver pulled into the pit area. Needless to say, speed was of necessity as was knowing where the tools were and being assured that they were. Our weekend race car enthusiast saw an immediate connection between his spare time activity and set-up reduction.

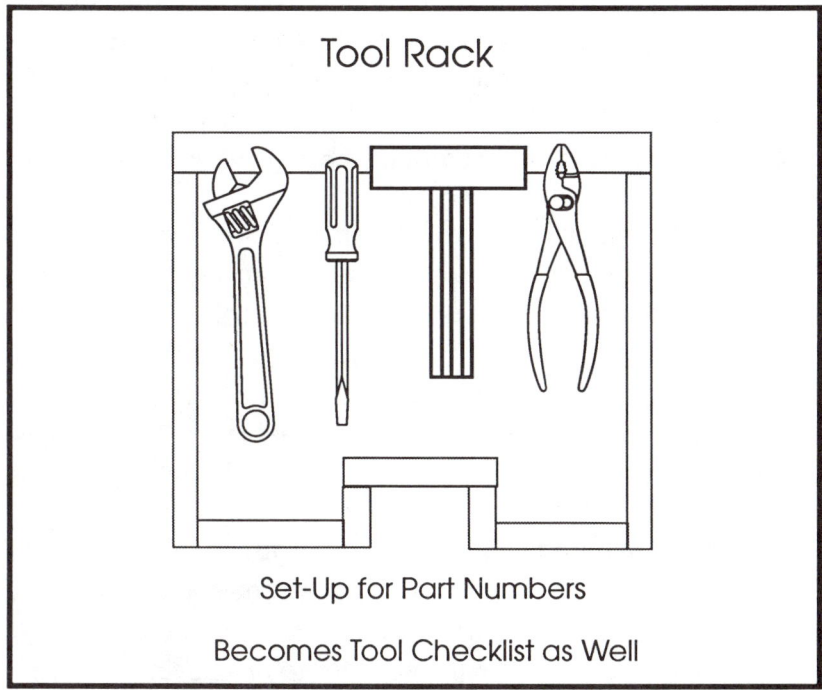

Tool Rack

Set-Up for Part Numbers

Becomes Tool Checklist as Well

"When that car comes in," he said in a team meeting one day, "I run to where the tire assembly and the air tool always are and I bring them out to the car. I always put the new tire down in the same spot. When I take the lug nuts off the wheel, I always put them down in the same spot. I know exactly where all my tools and materials are. It seems to me that set-up reduction would go faster if we could do something like what I do at the speedway here on the line."

Besides being an excellent example of a set-up reduction team doing its job well, this situation also demonstrates the two fundamental reasons for a tool rack in set-up reduction. When tools have a designated place, it greatly simplifies the task of finding the tool for the next job. Second, the tool rack itself becomes a tool checklist. A quick glance at the board will tell the employee if a tool is missing or not. And if a tool is missing, that means there is a problem to be resolved, before the changeover begins.

We also recommend that you begin to color code tools and fasteners. In other words, paint 1/2-inch wrenches and fasteners blue. Make 3/4-inch wrenches and fasteners red. Obviously, such a system eliminates the need for a set-up person or operator to measure or read dimensions. Be aware, however, that some people are color-blind. Other systems would have to be developed in these situations.

From a set-up standpoint, it would make sense for all fasteners to be of a uniform size so that only one size wrench or tool is needed for all operations. The ultimate in design, from a quick change perspective, is to eliminate the need for tools altogether. Whenever possible, design set-ups which use fasteners that come with a handle as part of the design. These fasteners can be tightened or loosened without spending any time looking for a tool.

CLAMPING REQUIREMENTS

While we are talking about fasteners, it makes sense to mention the clamping requirements for quick changeovers. As in the previous application, we first want to eliminate the need for tools when performing clamping operations. Second, we would like to use clamps which can be fastened down in one or, at most, two motions. Third, we need to identify where the stress forces are in an operation and how powerful they are. Often, for example, we clamp to prevent both side-to-side and up-down movement, when there are no up-down stress forces at all.

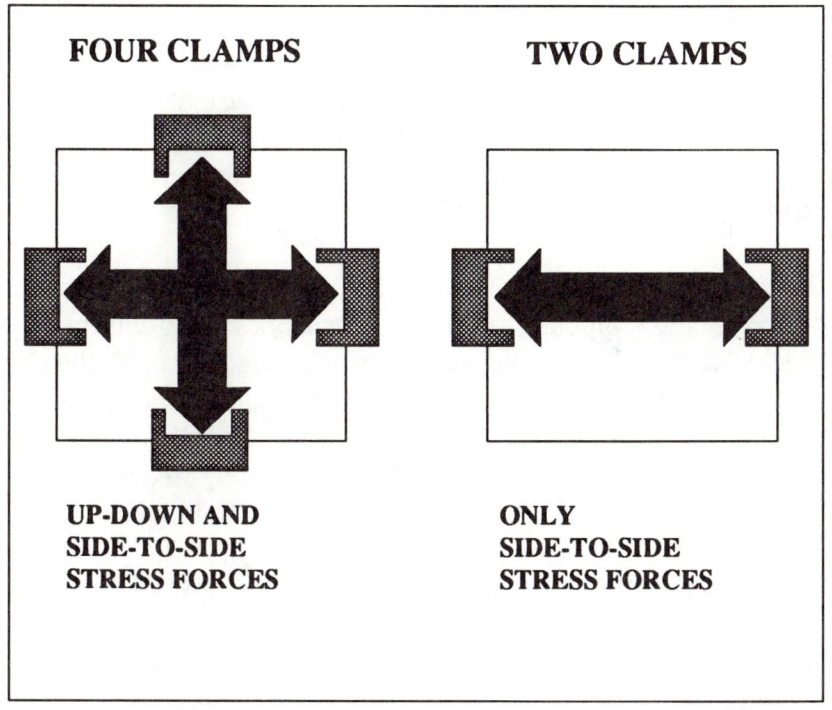

FOUR CLAMPS

TWO CLAMPS

UP-DOWN AND SIDE-TO-SIDE STRESS FORCES

ONLY SIDE-TO-SIDE STRESS FORCES

The set-up reduction rule is that if there are no stress forces, there is no reason to clamp. It follows then that if there are two less clamps, that the set-up can be completed in less time. Furthermore, we have found that many machines are "over-clamped." For example, a clamp capable of resisting a stress of 100 pounds is used where the stress never exceeds five pounds. A lighter clamp, in all likelihood, would do the job as well and would be easier to fasten (and would probably be less expensive). The use of a 1/4-turn fastener, for example, can greatly reduce set-up time. Granted, they won't work under extremely high stress, but they do work well for clamping, connecting and holding in place. The lesson here is to understand the stress forces so that you don't clamp where it is unnecessary.

DIE POSITIONING

One application which we witnessed was the use of v-blocks on a press in order to center dies on the equipment's bed. In the first step of this applications, two "v-blocks" were fastened to the work center as shown on the next page.

Before the dies were put into place, round stock was inserted between the "v-blocks" fastened to the work center and the "v-blocks" fastened to the die. All that was needed to center the die was to push the die forward. This action automatically centered the die from front to back and left to right. No adjustment was necessary. As the diagram shows, smaller dies required longer "v-blocks" attached; larger dies required shorter "v-blocks."

WORK CENTER CHANGEOVER GUIDES

A client of ours has a four-post press which requires tools weighing as much as two tons. At this company, the master

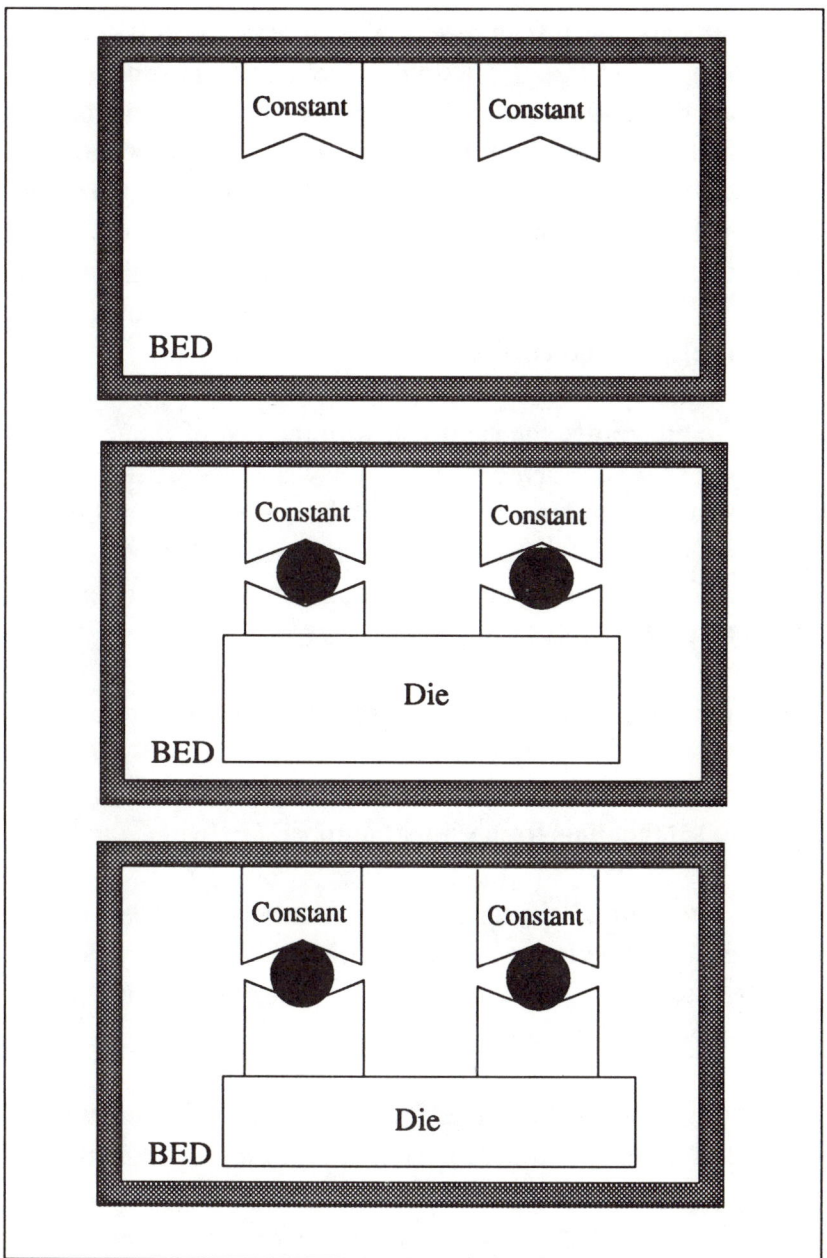

scheduler had never seen a set-up performed on this piece of equipment. It was through no fault of her own; she simply could never find time to get away from her office. Here, we thought, was the perfect person for the set-up reduction team on this machine. She has DSE, or a Different Set of Eyes. We knew her to be the type of person who would always ask "why?" It's people who ask "why" and who do not let accepted practices go unquestioned that we need. We were pleased that this master scheduler proved again that our selection process was valid.

At the first meeting, she sat down with the rest of the team and watched a videotape of the set-up. She saw the set-up person leave the press and go to his toolbox where he opened up a dog-eared spiral notebook and leafed through the pages. After locating the desired information, he put the notebook back and went over to the press and set the dials.

"What are you doing?" the master scheduler wanted to know.

"Over the years," the set-up person explained, "I've written down where to set the dials for each part number."

"That's interesting," she said, "but why don't we type them up and put them under plexiglass right next to the dials. That way, nobody has to walk back to their notebook. Everyone would know instantly what the settings should be."

Sure enough, the specifications for each part number were written on a chart under plexiglass next to the press the next time we visited the company. Not only was time saved because set-up people did not have to consult their notebooks, but now everybody

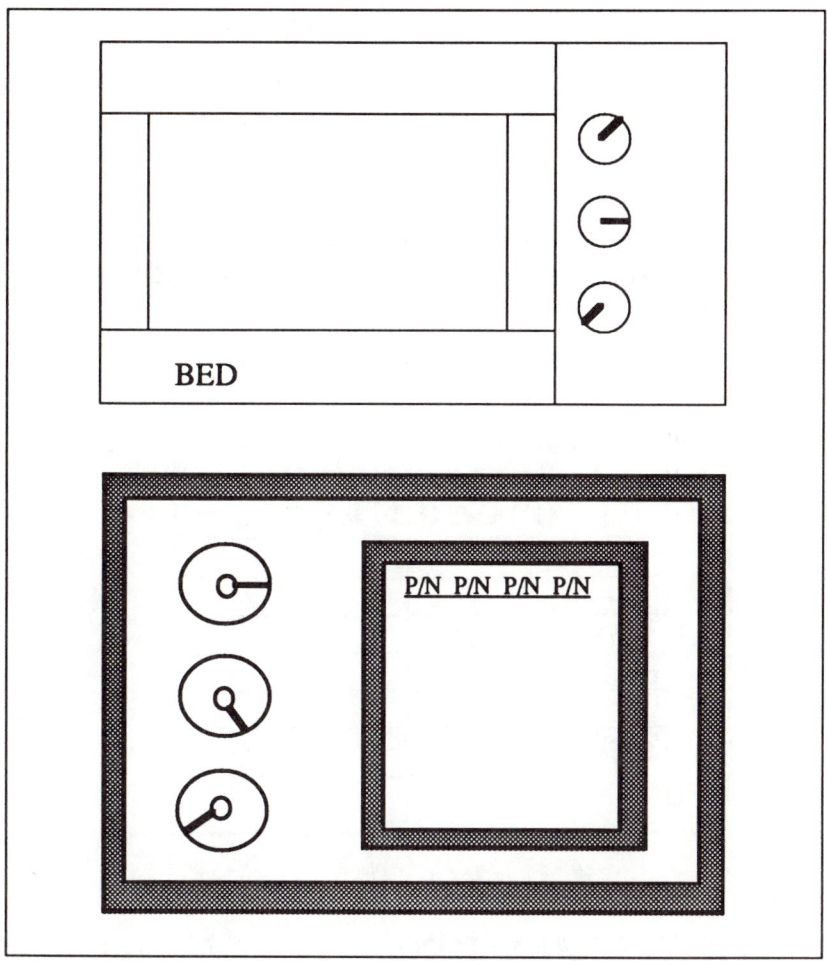

was using the same settings when setting up the machine. This can often mean a substantial improvement in quality. Lest we leave you with the impression that the set-up person in this example was not very imaginative, remember that he was the one who originally realized that some type of standardized measurement was necessary. After all, it was "the man on the floor," not management, who first started recording the settings. It simply took another "set of eyes," those of the master scheduler, to see that the settings would be of more use closer to the machine.

A set-up reduction team at General Foods solved a similar problem in the same way. The chart they developed listed optimum settings for the set-up person to follow. Again, this is a very easy solution to a persistent problem in all of our industries. Standardize the settings while making them easy to find and use.

Document Settings on Good Days	
Speed	
Feeds	
Temperature	
Fill Rate	
Etc...	
Etc...	

CRITICAL DIMENSIONS

A quick change team at General Foods solved a critical dimension problem in its set-up of a machine which filled feeder bowls with food products with a very simple, but effective technique. In this application, the set-up reduction team was attempting to find a way to adjust the chute height on a feeder tube (see diagram below) so that dusty products (chicken Florentine) would not sift away and so that bulky products (mushrooms) would not build up. It was just as detrimental for the critical dimension shown below to be too large as too small, depending on the product being fed into the bowl.

The first step was to standardize the chute tube adjustments for each different product and then to put markings at every 1/16 of an inch on the chute tube as the illustration shows. In the second step, the set-up reduction team decided to go to the machine shop and have gauges made for each different product. Now, instead of trying to "eyeball" the mark on the chute tube, the set-up person loosens a 1/4-turn fastener on the chute tube, puts the gauge into the area of the critical dimension, lowers or raises the chute tube and then tightens the fastener. It's no harder than gapping a spark plug.

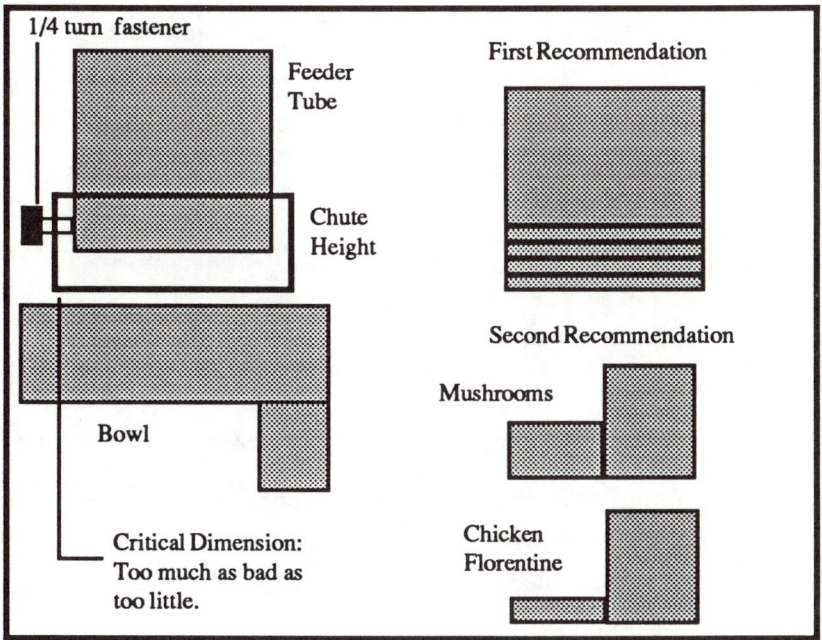

VACUUM BAGS

Here's another simple, but highly effective set-up application for vacuum bags which collect waste, dust and other environmentally hazardous particles. This is an effective technique for a number of different applications. At the company where we have encountered this solution, each of the twelve vacuum bags for a particular work center were individually attached. This meant that any time the bags had to be removed, the set-up person would have to loosen and eventually tighten as many as 15 different fasteners. The solution, as can be seen below, was to attach all twelve bags

to one aluminum grid which was then attached and loosened with two quick disconnect fasteners. Thus, when the frame was pulled off, all the vacuum bags came off as well and could be either cleaned or replaced as was necessary.

AUTOMATIC SHUT-OFFS

In this application, a manufacturer found that in the process of converting some of the internal operations of a changeover on a die press to external operations, defects were occurring where they had not before. It soon became apparent that the operator had, in the past, been responsible for watching that the die press punched a clean hole in the part. Now, however, the operator was busy getting the tools ready for the next changeover. Hence, a number of parts were being produced which had heavy burrs, slugs or dimples.

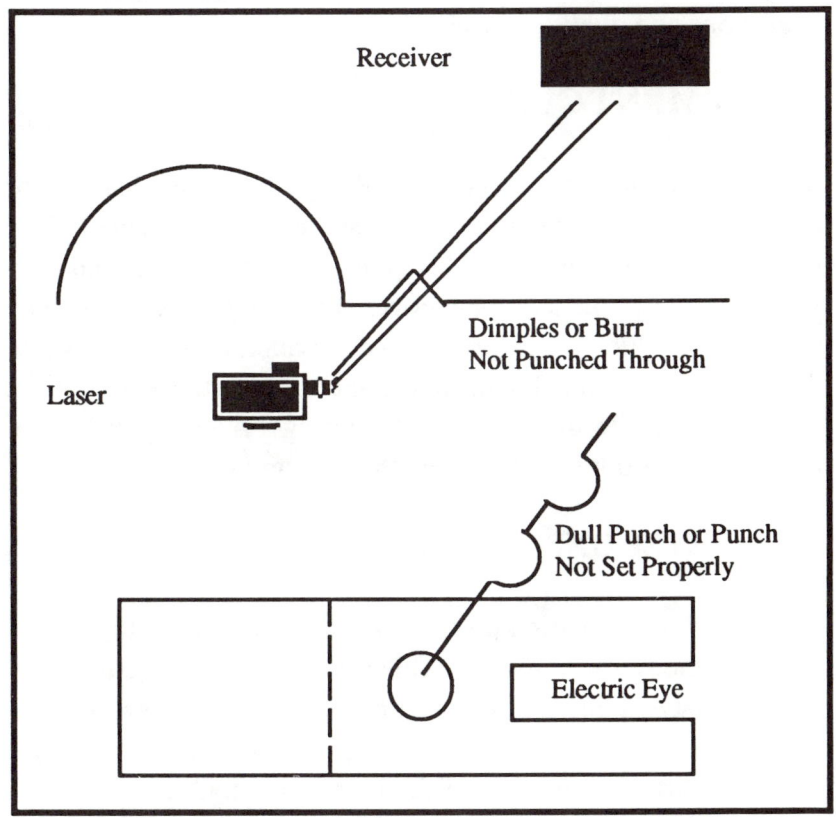

Instead of reverting to the procedures requiring the operator to watch the parts continuously, this company decided to solve the problem. The first step was to add an electronic eye to the press. Its function was to shut down the die press whenever light was unable to pass through the hole made by the die. That done, the set-up reduction team began to track the occurrences of defects. The tracking indicated that the defects could be eliminated by addressing the problems of dull and incorrectly set punches. In effect, this company was able to solve a quality problem and reduce changeover time with one action. This is an excellent example of how the benefits of set-up reduction often go beyond set-up and involve operations and quality as well.

EQUIPMENT CLEANING

Many companies are faced with the problem of cleaning or draining product out of surge bins and screw conveyors before making a different product. This quite obviously adds a considerable amount of time to a changeover. The problem is how to take a procedure which has always been done internally (that is, when the machine is shut down) and make it an external operation (performed while the machine is running). A set-up reduction team at one of our clients solved the problem in this way:

STEP ONE

Put a transition piece in between the surge bin and the screw conveyor. This transition piece should have a quick disconnect mechanism so an operator can quickly remove the piece as soon as the surge bin empties of the first product. Once removed, the operator then cleans the surge bin and closes the cut-off gate while the screw conveyor is emptying itself of the product.

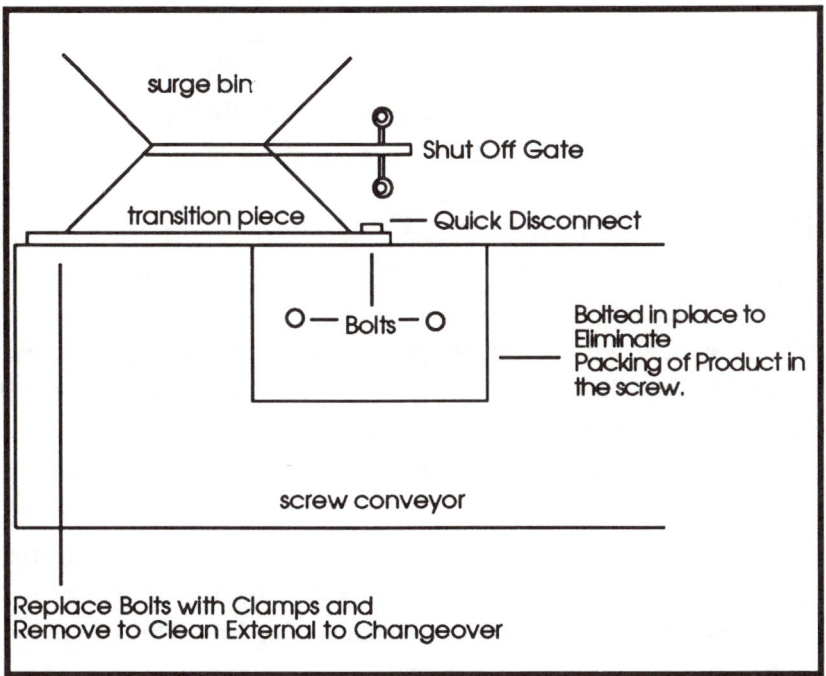

STEP TWO

As the surge bin begins to fill with the next product, the operator begins cleaning the screw conveyor. Once he completes this operation, he can then put the transition piece back in place and the line is ready to roll.

This set-up reduction team also went on to explore a quicker way to clean the screw conveyor. At their last meeting, they were discussing how to build a squeegee with rubber blades which could be clamped on to the screw conveyor. The screw could then clean itself as it made its last few revolutions.

As a general rule, you should always do cleaning operations external to the set-up. Another method is to duplicate the parts which need cleaning, sterilization or sanitization.

DOWNTIME ELIMINATION

In process industries, set-up time is often lengthened because the filler must stop when the packaging line is changed over for a new streamer of product. At a food-processing client, they eliminated the downtime on the filler line in two stages. Originally product was stored in pouch streamers which were placed in drums.

In the first stage of the team's improvement process, the drums were placed on rollers in order to facilitate the movement of the product from the filling line to the packaging line. This improvement, however, still did not meet the goal of moving the product directly from the filling line to the packaging line without storing it in drums. One very big obstacle still needed to be overcome: If there was any downtime on the filling line, the packaging line would shut down because it would stop receiving product.

The solution was to eliminate the drums and to utilize the coil surge principle which basically acts as a surge bin. The product from the filling line fills up the coil of the floop before it reaches the packaging line.

Now, whenever the filling line stops to introduce a new streamer of product, the packaging line doesn't have to stop as well. The packaging line simply uses the material which has built up in the surge. This principle allows for filler downtime and for the attachment of new streamers of product during changeover. We have also used this principle in the fabric and coil steel industries. In the case of the fabric industry, the surge contains one type of material which is used by the current operation while the new type of material is stapled on the end of the roll of the old material. Likewise for coil steel where the different coils are welded together to maintain a continuous feed from the line in the surge.

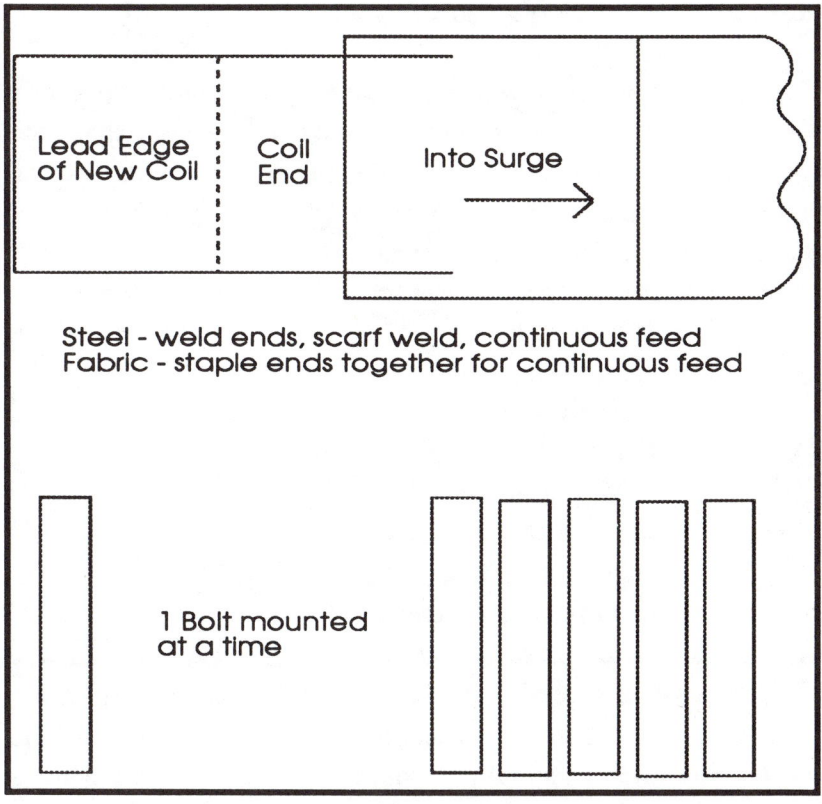

OFFICE APPLICATIONS

It is not uncommon for the principles of set-up reduction to be applied to all areas of a company. For example, one client videotaped the processing of invoices for payment. Their goal was not only to reduce make-ready time, but reduce processing time as well. While watching the videotape, the team came up with many ideas: move the files closer to the user, organize the rubber stamps, consolidate phone calls, etc. And then, one team member who had obviously learned our lesson which teaches members to ask "Why? Why? Why? Why? Why?," stood up and asked the most important question. "Why do we process invoices?"

The answer was to resolve errors. The next obvious question was "Why not eliminate the errors?" To make a long story short, the company eventually eliminated over 90 percent of its invoice processing. The team went to Purchasing and asked them to get accurate information on the purchase order for:

- **Part number.**
- **Quantity.**
- **Description.**
- **Price.**
- **FOB point.**
- **Freight payment terms.**
- **Discount terms.**
- **Supplier name and address.**

They then asked receiving to verify the accuracy of the packing slip, including the purchase order number. Once this was done, the company notified its suppliers that there was no longer any need to send invoices. The accounting department now attaches the packing slip to a copy of the purchase order and pays according to the terms on the P.O. The three clerks formerly processing invoices are now working in another, more productive area.

Another office application occurred at Kawasaki. We were working on eliminating duplicate files and decided that purchase orders were an obvious place to start. Why have a file in Receiving, another in Purchasing and yet another in Accounting? Proper use of the computer open order system allowed us to maintain a hard copy file only in Accounting and to free two clerical people for four hours per day for more productive work.

At a manufacturing client, we videotaped a customer service employee receiving and entering a customer order over the phone. Simply by asking "Why?" and "How could we?," the set-up reduction team reduced the time needed to complete the task by over 40 percent. There are times when a videotape is not possible or necessary. In that event, we tell clients to use the "Swallow Test."

Does what you are seeing or hearing make sense (or perhaps better "cents")?

If the answer is "yes," then it passes the test. If the answer is "no," then it does not pass and must be corrected or eliminated.

Perhaps it was the "Swallow Test" which was recently used at the Pentagon. Looking at their process of issuing licenses, somebody asked a very simple question. "Why," that person said, "do we give all these people tests and issue driving licenses when they already have state-issued licenses? Why are we even issuing licenses?" The answer to the "Swallow Test" for this situation was a definite "no." The Pentagon will have saved hundreds of thousands of dollars by eliminating this unnecessary practice.

CHAPTER TEN

DESIGN FOR PRODUCIBILITY: QUICK CHANGE OBJECTIVES

In order to reduce changeover time on machinery, equipment and product designers as well as manufacturing personnel must work together during the design phase. Manufacturers know what they want — small lots and quick changes — and designers can make them possible. Together, they must design for one touch changeovers. Some of the areas at which they should be looking in order to reduce changeover time are listed on the next page.

- Quick change tooling — tools should be designed for specific use during changeover.
- Elimination of hand tools.
- Elimination of adjustments — machine parts should lock into predetermined positions.
- Quick die changes.
- Clean-up reduction or external clean-up — as in the food processing, cosmetic or printing industries where food, nail polish or inks must be flushed out of the system.

One of the most important features of quick change is the ability to design parts or products which can be produced at the lowest total cost and the highest possible quality without going through a lengthy and costly changeover. The typical process of product development goes through a sequence such as the one depicted here:

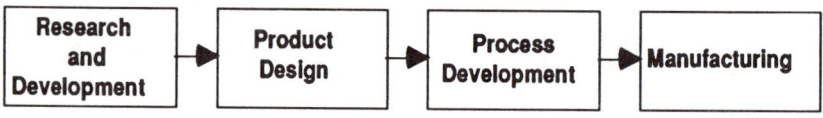

The new process of product development in which a company designs for producibility looks much different. First of all, note in the diagram on the next page that the process is a circular, as opposed to a linear sequence. This is because the DFP (Design for Producibility) process continuously seeks to improve quality and eliminate waste.

```
┌──────────────┐      ┌──────────────┐      ┌──────────────┐
│  Marketing   │ ───▶ │   Establish  │ ───▶ │   Product    │
│   Concept    │      │Design & Process     │  and Process │
│              │      │    Rules     │      │    Design    │
└──────────────┘      └──────────────┘      └──────────────┘
       ▲                                            │
       │                                            ▼
       │                                     ┌──────────────┐
       │                                     │  Analysis of │
       │                                     │ Quick Change │
       │                                     │  Techniques  │
       │                                     └──────────────┘
       │                                            │
┌──────────────┐                                    ▼
│   Analysis   │      ┌──────────────────────────────────────┐
│     of       │ ◀─── │            Producibility             │
│ Manufacturing│      └──────────────────────────────────────┘
└──────────────┘
```

Note also that product and process design are now done at the same time in order to assure that the designed product can indeed be produced in the most cost-effective manner possible and with the highest quality and shortest set-up time.

The advantages of doing product and process design according to the DFP concept are as follows:

- Lower labor, material and overhead costs.
- Reduced tooling costs.
- Fewer number of parts.
- Increased flexibility in manufacturing.
- Earlier product development.
- Products designed for quality. (Make it right the first time.)

These advantages can be best achieved by setting objectives and developing strategies in which a product design team, consisting of people from engineering, manufacturing and from the suppliers of material or parts, resolves problems early in the design process. Let's look now at the design stages in the DFP process.

DESIGN REQUIREMENTS AND RULES

The primary requirement is to establish product design teams and to train employees to use the rules below in coming up with their own solutions to tooling, equipment, product and production problems. The purpose of a DFP team in quick change is to solve problems early in the design process before large amounts of money, time or other resources have been used or committed. This is where a Computer Aided Design (CAD) system comes into its own. CAD systems are designed to allow users to try "what if" solutions. A CAD system allows a company to ask questions like "What if we made the product from a different material?", "What if we changed this dimension?", etc. and see the repercussions of that decision. This does not mean, of course, that a company can't apply the design rules below if it does not own a CAD system:

- Use fewer components or assemblies.
- Eliminate fasteners.
- Strive for simple designs.
- Design for testing, not inspection.
- Reduce complexity.
- Utilize the plug and play concept (modular design).
- Establish quick change technology.
- Employ the top-down assembly rule.
- Design for one surface processing.
- Minimize hidden pockets.
- Use snap together designs.
- Standardize components.

The guiding principle behind all these rules and requirements of DFP is really very simple. The principle says that the best designed part and tooling is no part or tool at all and that the best designed process is no process at all. In essence, this is a "zero-defect" philosophy for design. If a company designs a machine, process or product right the first time, it will make the product right the first time and every time.

Now let's look in more detail at some of the design rules above in order to see exactly how a company can design for producibility. **Component, tooling and process reduction** is one certain way to simplify designs and to make production easier. These are some of the areas that we suggest you look at when working on this design problem:

- Minimize part counts.
- Incorporate one part with another.
- Use implosion techniques. (The classic example is taking six battery caps that are screw fastening and coming up with two caps that are snap fit.)
- Use multifunctional components. (One design fits all.)

Another design rule is called the **"plug and play" or modular design concept.** The rationale behind modular design is to create as few parts as possible so that both sub-assembly and final assembly will be more simple. Hence, there will be far fewer quality issues to resolve as parts are tested during the actual process instead of inspecting after they are finished. Fewer parts will also result in reduced inventory and quality improvements will mean fewer field problems.

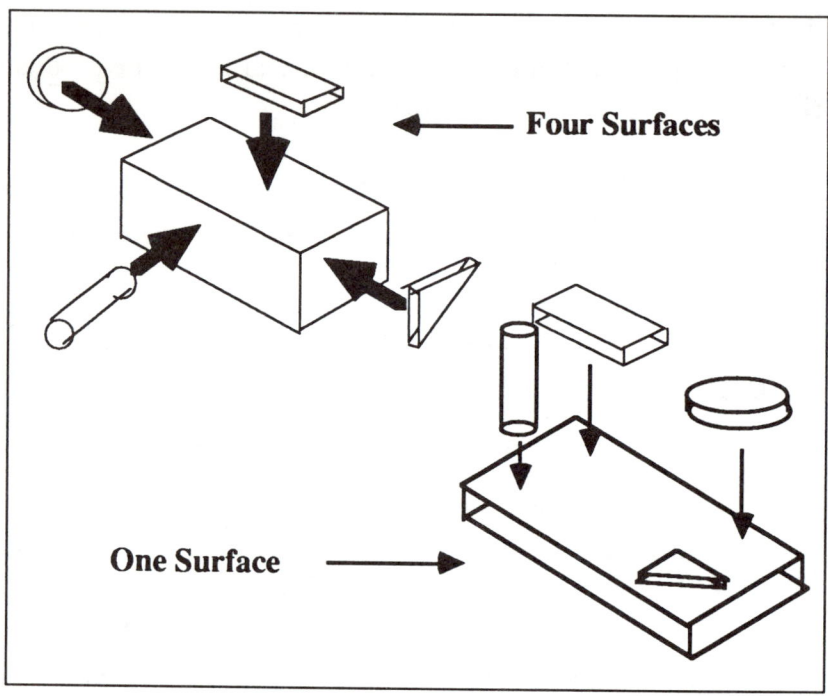

Reducing the number of surfaces to process, or **one surface processing,** will eliminate expensive part orientation by a machine or operator. Some cube-shaped products, for example, attach components to all six sides. This means that the product must be turned six times before it is complete. Using DFP rules, however, it is possible to design the same process so that all the components are on one surface. Now the product can flow through the process or production line without ever being rotated. This eliminates wasted motion, allows for the visual inspection and identification of the product, introduces same direction assembly and improves the process flow.

Closely linked to the DFP rule above is the need to **minimize hidden pockets**. This not only improves visual checking by the operator, but, in many cases, simply makes it easier for an operator to work on components which used to be in hard-to-get places. Anybody who has worked on a car engine has a good idea of what this design rule can eliminate.

Whenever possible, use **simple, snap-together designs** in which different fixtures, tools or components fit together without the need for fasteners or adjustments. This technique will not streamline automated tooling changes, but it will reduce the cost of changeover by a considerable amount as all torquing of components is eliminated.

Lastly, there is **component standardization** which is probably the single most powerful DFP principle at your disposal. If you are able to design process, tooling and products that all use the same components, except in different configurations, then you would be able to use the same equipment to produce all the products without the need for extensive set-ups. Some companies have moved toward this by first standardizing one part of their product. A housewares manufacturer, for example, began component standardization by making all the covers for its pans of the same size. Now, they need only one machine to make all their covers, instead of one machine for each size cover.

These are only some of the DFP techniques which a company can employ as it designs a product. Since engineers and designers don't have to go through a time-consuming drawing stage, there is actually more time for them to review a design, to see if they can find a design which will be easier to produce and which will reduce set-up times.

CONCLUSION

DFP is a new technology which is garnering a tremendous amount of interest today. Although little has been written so far about the tooling process and changes required, we are sure that there will be many seminars, articles and books which will shed some light on this opportunity. Ultimately, DFP will tie into "time to market" and thus allow companies to compete far more successfully in the world market. Peter L. Grieco, Jr, Pro-Tech CEO and founder, states that "the future is in applying DFP rules — *today!* "

CHAPTER ELEVEN

CONTINUOUS IMPROVEMENT

Now that you have acquired the tools and the knowledge to implement a set-up reduction program, bear in mind that you should not be pleased with your initial successes. Early successes must not be accepted as completion of the process. There is no greater disappointment in the world of business than being witness to a company that implements a pilot set-up reduction program and then fails to capitalize on its results by expanding the process. It's like qualifying for the Olympics and then deciding not to compete. Improvement is a continuous process which strives for World Class status and, once there, explores more efficient and flexible methods for manufacturing components which meet all of the customer's specifications and demands, 100 percent of the time.

A company's major objective, after the set-up reduction program has been implemented, is to avoid being a "one-shot" phenomenon, like the rookie pitcher who wins 20 games in his first season and is never heard from again. What's it going to take to be the company that doesn't fizzle out? It will take dedication at all levels of the company to ensure meeting the objectives. We believe that following the **THREE E's** will keep a company moving in the right direction:

Set-up reduction must be fun in order to gain employee involvement. But to have fun requires a lot of **energy**, and hard work, in the areas of education, training and teambuilding in order to make the program succeed. And when it succeeds, that's when the rewards and **excitement** come from seeing the results of hard work. It's exciting to see measurement graphs of set-up time and lot sizes turn down and stay down. It's exciting to see warehouses emptied as inventory levels recede. Finally, all the energy and excitement results from **experience**, the experience which is gained from working on a project and knowing why it succeeded. This means that a company can continue to build on its experience by spreading its past successes throughout the facility and organization. We call this process "Cloning for Success."

EXPANDING THE PROGRAM — PILOT TO CIP

The primary responsibility for capitalizing on the successful results of a pilot implementation of set-up reduction rests with the steering committee. Its role is to create and manage teams as well as to facilitate. A steering committee reviews progress and decides when to form new teams. There are three ways to create a new team:

- **Start from scratch (all new players).**

- **Germinate a team with a seed from one of the existing teams.**

- **Transplant an existing team into a new project area.**

If care was taken to select motivated and qualified individuals on the pilot project, then none of these various ways to propagate new teams should be difficult. Furthermore, teams must get up to speed much more quickly than the pilot teams since the company has already progressed along the learning curve. In other words, new teams will not need to travel cautiously over territory that is now well known. Keep in mind, however, that speed is counterproductive if it just makes for more mistakes. Ask yourself: Is faster better, or is better faster? A steady plan for improvement should be developed.

THE SUPERVISOR'S ROLE
— CULTURE CHANGE

In Chapter Six, we mentioned that the front line supervision was the cornerstone of a set-up reduction program. They are also the foundation for the Continuous Improvement Process. In general, supervisors must adopt a "Get Good" attitude instead of a "Get Tough" attitude. They should not be swinging baseball bats to get people's attention, but should be asking people to do what comes naturally — to improve performance. Supervisors are the people who direct the company's set-up reduction program on the floor. Here are some of the rules they will need to folllow:

- **Supervisors must insist on problem identification from operators and set-up people as soon as indicated.**

- **Superviors must respect the ideas and opinions of all others who are trying to identify and solve problems.**

- **Supervisors must ensure that procedures, policies and methods are followed.**

- **Supervisors must insist that measurements be kept daily or weekly.**

- Supervisors must demand that all equipment be kept in a perfect state of repair.

- Supervisors must demand a safe environment and adherence to safety procedures.

- Supervisors must ensure that employee contracts are not violated.

- Supervisors must develop means for rewarding success.

TRAINING AND EDUCATION

Companies which seek to improve themselves through an ongoing process must insure that training and education are continuous as well. Supervisors play another important role in this area as the principal means of identifying educational and training needs. Certainly additional teams will need to be taught the same subjects we recommended in Chapter Six for pilot teams. These areas once again are:

- Total Business Concepts.
- Teambuilding techniques.
- Set-up reduction techniques.
- Problem-solving techniques.
- Operator training (in order to standardize machine work).
- Statistical Process Control.

MEASUREMENTS AND CONTROLS

We measure to establish the present base. In the case of set-up time, we would measure in order to determine how long it takes to set up now. If we were measuring lot sizes, we would count the present number of parts per lot produced. Once a base is established, we use measurements to monitor our progress toward a goal. Set-up time, for example, should move toward the goal of a 75 percent low-cost/no-cost reduction in time. Lot sizes should move toward a goal where the quantity is small enough to allow

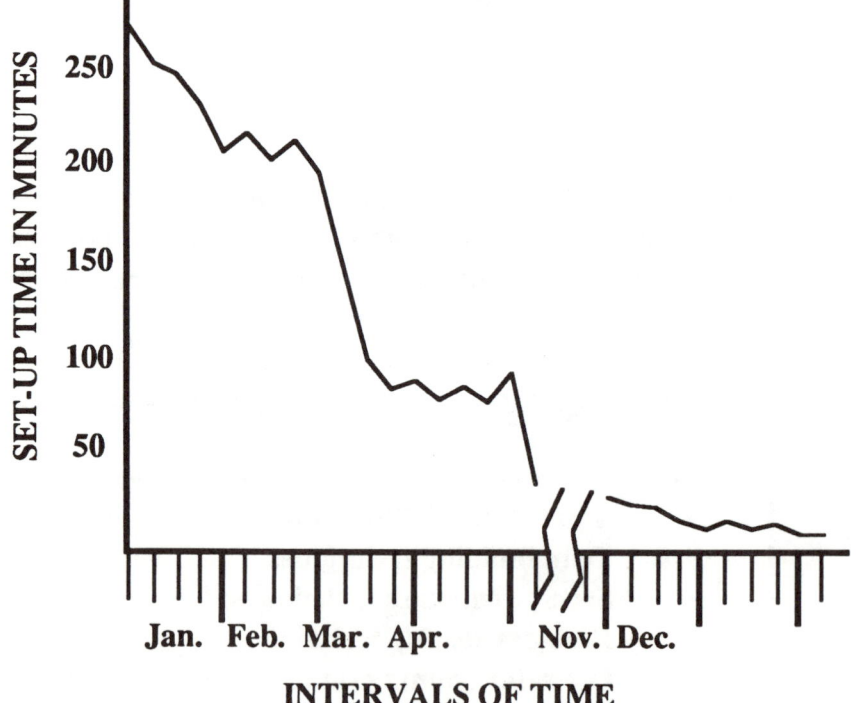

**SET-UP REDUCTION
MEASUREMENT GRAPH**

manufacturing to produce the quantity ordered by customers. Ideally, we should strive for a lot size of one.

Perhaps most importantly measurements are useful as a dynamic management tool which establishes a results orientation in the workplace. A measurement graph like the one on the previous page 1for set-up time should be displayed throughout the plant for each factor you plan to measure. What is being measured (set-up time) should appear on the vertical axis and the intervals of time (weeks) along the horizontal axis. By the way, we recommend that you make measurements either weekly or monthly, preferably weekly. Daily, on the other hand, may be too frequent and quarterly is not frequent enough.

You will find that the partial list on the next page is a starting point for a company to begin measurements in a set-up reduction program. Remember that staying on top of measuring often requires a change in focus. For instance, some measurements used early in the program such as set-up time may be replaced by lot size measurements later in the program. Also, be aware that different work centers in the factory have undergone set-up reduction for a number of different reasons. One center, for example, may have had a problem with maintenance. Set-up time may be meaningless on this machine whereas the number of repairs would be of vital importance.

At General Foods' Stovetop Stuffing line, for example, the set-up reduction team originally published measurement graphs for uptime, compliance to schedule, ZDQR (Zero Defect Quality Rating) and rework. Eventually, rework was no longer measured because it no longer existed.

SUGGESTED SET-UP MEASUREMENTS

- **Set-up time (minutes).**
- **Cost vs. Savings.**
- **Uptime (minutes).**
- **Number of set-ups performed.**
- **Lot size reduction.**
- **Compliance to schedule.**
- **Salvage or rework.**
- **Finished goods quality.**
- **Scrap generation.**
- **Customer service level.**
- **Dollars of inventory (Purchased, Work-In-Process, Finished Goods, MRO—Maintenance, Repair and Operating)**
- **Puchased material quality.**
- **Set-up scrap.**
- **Start-up time (time to reach normal efficiency).**
- **Internal Set-up vs. External Set-up.**
- **Total cost measurement by department.**

ROADBLOCKS TO CIP

Below are twenty-one of our favorite excuses for why set-up reduction won't work and why continuous improvement is impossible. No matter which plant we assist, the reasons are the same.

It doesn't matter if the company has sales in the billions or the several hundred thousands, whether it's union or non-union, whether it's process, repetitive or discrete. Set-up reduction and continuous improvement are always impossible for companies which say the following:

1. WE TRIED IT BEFORE. (35 years ago)
2. OUR COMPANY IS DIFFERENT.
3. IT'S NOT MY JOB.
4. WE'RE TOO BUSY.
5. WE'VE NEVER DONE IT BEFORE.
6. IT'S AGAINST COMPANY POLICY.
7. IT'S NOT REALISTIC.
8. IT'S NOT A PROBLEM NOW.
9. WE'RE NOT READY FOR THAT NEW-FANGLED STUFF.
10. WE DIDN'T PUT IT IN THE BUDGET.
11. LET'S THINK ABOUT IT FOR AWHILE.
12. WE GOT WHERE WE ARE WITHOUT IT.
13. LET'S START A COMMITTEE TO STUDY IT.
14. OUR CUSTOMERS WON'T LIKE IT.
15. IT WON'T WORK IN OUR INDUSTRY.
16. YOU GUYS ARE TEN YEARS AHEAD OF YOUR TIME.
17. WHY CHANGE IT IF IT'S STILL WORKING?
18. LET'S DO SOME MARKET RESEARCH FIRST.
19. WHAT ARE OUR COMPETITORS DOING?
20. TELL US WHAT TO DO TO OUR EQUIPMENT.
21. WE LIKE YOUR IDEAS, BUT ...

Our reply is consistent and simple. If you don't start improving your company right now, your competitors are still going to improve their companies. Two years from now, when you are packing up your belongings, your competitors will have one less company to worry about.

GENERAL CIP PRINCIPLES

Assisting in a great number of set-up reduction programs has enabled us to observe many common prinicples. These principles can be used to reduce set-up time for any type of application. The first set of guidelines are ten prinicples of common-sense motion:

PRINCIPLES OF COMMON-SENSE MOTION

1. Use both hands whenever possible.
2. Use simultaneous hand motions as often as possible.
3. Keep hand and arm motions short.
4. Avoid sharp changes in direction of movements.
5. Slide objects instead of picking them up.
6. Establish and maintain a rhythm.
7. Use fasteners or clamps to hold objects in order to free hands.
8. Store material near work center.
9. Prearrange tools and parts.
10. Locate machine controls for ease of operation.

The principles above often lead to the following improvements at a work center. Consider these applications in your own company:

COMMON IMPROVEMENTS

1. Install gravity delivery chutes.
2. Use drop delivery.
3. Compare methods if more than one set-up person performs the job.
4. Use air ejection.
5. Do two at a time.
6. Improve jigs or fixtures by providing ejectors, quick-disconnect clamps, etc.
7. Use foot-operated mechanisms.
8. Arrange for a two-handed operation.
9. Combine machines or operations to eliminate idle time.
10. Utilize improvements developed for other work centers.
11. Eliminate fasteners.
12. Eliminate line-up by using fixed stops.
13. Eliminate hand tools.
14. Standardize settings.
15. Use pictures instead of words in procedure manuals.

The best set-up is no set-up at all. It is important for a company to also ask itself some searching questions about the necessity of an operation or a process. If operations or processes can be combined, then the number of required set-ups decreases and, obviously, the overall set-up time for a work center or production line. The following questions about the purpose of an operation and an analysis of a process are vital to continuous improvement in a set-up reduction program:

WHAT IS THE PURPOSE
OF THE SET-UP SEGMENT OR ELEMENT?

- Is the accomplished result necessary?
- What makes it necessary?
- Does the operation correct a difficulty experienced in an earlier operation?
- Does it correct the difficulty?
- Has the performance of the previous segment or element been subsequently corrected?
- If the segment or element is done to improve the appearance, is the cost justified?
- Can the supplier of the material perform the segment or element more economically?
- Can the design be changed to eliminate the purpose of the segment or element?
- Is the segment or element done to satisfy the requirements of all customers or just one? Or only a few?
- Would adding another segment or element make it easier to perform this one?
- Can this segment or element be combined with another?
- Can the segment or element be eliminated by changing the procedure?
- Can it be subdivided and the various parts added to other operations?

- Can part of the segment or element be performed more effectively as a separate segment?
- Can the segment or element be performed during the idle period of another segment?
- Is the sequence of operations the best possible?
- Can the set-up be performed more economically on a different machine?
- Can the segment or element and its inspection be combined?
- If parts were of 100 percent quality, would inspection be necessary?

Keep these principles and questions in mind in order to maintain the improvement process started by the implementation of a set-up reduction program. Now let's review how other companies have applied these principles and the principles of set-up reduction developed earlier in the book to various applications.

CHAPTER TWELVE

$AVING DOLLARS
WITH COMMON SENSE

The case studies in this chapter are included to provide you with examples of what other companies have accomplished with their set-up reduction programs. As we have worked with these companies, we have learned one very important lesson. That lesson is that we can learn from others even if they are not in the same industry. We hope you keep an open mind as you read this chapter and discover techniques that will apply at your company. Note also the suggestions for teambuilding and team management as well as an overall sense of how to implement and maintain the program. Most of all, we think you will come away with the enthusiasm to start your company's program. The results recorded here are real and tangible in monetary terms. They are results that you can attain with the right mind-set. Set-up reduction applies to more than punch presses and milling machines.

BENDIX
FRICTION MATERIALS DIVISION
Troy, New York and Cleveland, Tennessee

Set-up reduction teams can accomplish significant reductions in machine changeover times using our simple, practical and inexpensive methodologies. This is exactly what happened when teams were established at the Friction Materials Division of Bendix in Cleveland, TN, and Troy, NY. With Project Engineer Joe Bedard acting as a facilitator and manager, these teams were able to reduce a particular set-up from 12 hours to 1 hour and 10 minutes. Still another set-up went from 65 minutes to 12 minutes. What is most surprising is that most of these reductions were the result of a "first pass" at the problem. In other words, further reductions are possible. The only constraint now is whether Bendix feels that cost analysis will justify a further reduction.

These results are even more phenomenal when it is realized that as little as $700 was spent on reducing the set-up time on one machine by over 80 percent. Plant Manager Jay Patel (Troy, NY) reports that other set-up reduction efforts were accomplished well below budget.

Despite more than satisfactory results in reducing set-up time at relatively low costs, Bendix feels that the major advantage of set-up reduction has been to increase production capacity at a time when customer demand has risen sharply. Both the Cleveland and Troy plants make disk and drum brakes for the automotive and aerospace industries. New FAA regulations have required airlines to change brakes more frequently and thus buy more replacements from Bendix and other manufacturers. In fact, demand shot up by 50 percent at Bendix which then faced the problem of how to increase capacity without accruing significant expenses.

The solution was to identify those machines which caused production constraints, or bottlenecks, and to attack the set-up time of each. A reduction in set-up time would allow for smaller lot sizes and, most importantly, greater flexibility whether it was JIT or not. Several kinds of brakes could then be produced in order to meet customer demand. In other words, Bendix was looking to build today what it sold yesterday in order to attain 100 percent customer service.

The following examples will describe the process of each machine before set-up reduction was performed. We will then note what set-up reduction principles were used and how they were applied in order to reduce changeover time.

The Briquette Press

The Briquette press is responsible for producing front disc brake pads which are sold to U.S. Auto manufacturers and to Toyota. Basically, the machine indexes to various stations where the pad material and the backing material are dispensed and compressed. The finished unit is then sent on to an oven for the final hardening.

The process begins when a hopper dispenses a predetermined

amount of backing material on to a conveyor. The conveyor then drops the material into a mold on a turntable. The turntable indexes to the first station where a tamping foot compresses the material. After indexing again, the turntable rotates the compressed material in the mold to the second station where a metallic compound is dropped on top of the backing material. The mold is then indexed to a third station where, like the first station, a tamp foot compresses the metallic compound. At the fourth station, the newly formed briquette is ejected from the mold and goes down a chute where it waits to be brought to the hardening oven.

For every different kind of brake pad, each station had to be removed and adjusted during the set-up. The original set-up (before any improvements) took 65 minutes. Because some automation had been added to the machine, the control panel which indexed the turntable was located away from the area where the set-up person was doing his job. Therefore, for every removal and adjustment, the set-up person had to walk around the machine to get at the control panel. One of the first ideas which the set-up team implemented was moving the control panel back to the area where the set-up person operated.

After receiving training from Mike Gozzo, Executive Vice President and co-founder of ProTech, Joe Bedard and the set-up team used the videotape method and observed that there were well over 50 bolts which had to be loosened, removed and then tightened again. Many of these bolts were not very accessible. The tamp foot for the backing material used to be composed of 5 parts. By simplifying the design of this tool, the set-up team was able to reduce the number of parts to one. Furthermore, the team placed two ratcheting handles on the tamp foot. All it takes to release or lock the piece now is a one-half turn.

The bolts holding the tamp foot in place were also replaced with one-third turn fasteners. These fasteners allow the set-up person to remove the tamp foot without disconnecting the entire assembly. Before set-up reduction, the height of the tamp foot was determined by "touch-feel-go" adjusting by the set-up person. The team decided to eliminate adjustment by presetting the height of the tamp foot for each different kind of brake pad. No more adjustment was needed. It should be noted here that the changes which occurred at the tamping station for the backing material were also implemented at the tamping station for the metallic compound. Thus, one solution resolved two problems.

The team also found a need for scheduled preventive maintenance on the Briquette press. They decided to replace a quarter-century-old hydraulic pump for which they couldn't get any spare parts with a centrifugal pump. In doing so, the team also replaced the bolts which held the pump in place with quick-disconnects. It now takes only three minutes to remove a pump and replace it with a new one. This time is short enough that Bendix instituted a policy whereby a pump, whether it was functioning correctly or not, would be changed every three months and returned to the manufacturer for an overhaul. Although not strictly set-up reduction, this action aided in reducing downtime during a set-up because of pumps which did not function correctly.

While viewing a videotape of the set-up, the team noticed that the set-up person was often looking for tools. He had a tool cart but because of the configuration of the machines, he was unable to bring it close to the Briquette press. The team solved this problem by changing the truck's configuration so that it would now fit into the area where the set-up person was working.

This tool cart also carried a replacement set of scales for weighing the material which comprised the part. This scale was already calibrated so that it could just slide into the place where the previous scale had been. The amount of times that this was necessary was also reduced by simply maintaining the presently used scales. The team made it mandatory that the electronics of each scale had to be cleaned. This alone greatly improved their function.

Addressing a clean-up problem was one set-up principle that the set-up teams used consistently to standardize the set-up procedures. The team observed that one set-up person cleaned up his area after every step in the operation. At first glance, this may seem desirable since well-maintained machines last longer and produce parts of far superior quality. However, this person's cleanliness was beyond what was necessary and also different from the procedures on the other two shifts. The team decided at that point that it was necessary to standardize and document the set-up so that it was performed in one way. This greatly helped in the education and training of new set-up people. Bendix now supplies laminated "cue" cards to new set-up people. Doing so means that set-up time does not skyrocket whenever a new person takes over from an experienced person.

The team also saw that this particular set-up person was very careful because, at each step, he did not have the proper tools to perform an adequate clean-up. The team arranged for improved vacuum ductwork to be brought to the machine and for attachments which would allow the set-up person to get into corners and such.

FOCUSED VACUUM DUCTWORK

All of these set-up reduction techniques, which cost approximately $700 to implement, resulted in a reduction of over 80 percent in set-up time (from 65 minutes to 12 minutes).

The Segment Drill

The Segment drill takes a brake shoe pad and puts it in multi-head drilling machine with five independent drilling heads. Here, too, most of the time reduction came in eliminating adjustments and reducing the types and numbers of bolts. These types of quick change techniques resulted in the set-up time being lowered to 1 hour and 10 minutes from an original time of 12 hours.

The first step taken by the team was to eliminate the different sizes and types of bolts. The set-up person used hex, ratchet and even open-end wrenches to fit over eight different sizes. It's not hard to imagine the time spent looking for the right tool each time when there were 96 different bolts for a total of 192 tightenings and loosenings. There are now 2 different kinds of bolts which resulted in a 1 hour reduction by itself. A further reduction was achieved by using an air wrench.

Another reduction was achieved by making the adjustment of the drill depth an external set-up operation, that is, an operation which occurs while the machine is operating. Drill depths for the next job are set while the present job is running. This segment is facilitated by another set-up reduction in the removal of the shroud which covers each drill head. One team member asked why screws were needed to hold the five shrouds in place. It was determined that they indeed weren't needed and were replaced by two ball-lock pins.

On this set-up reduction effort, as with others, there was a need to standardize and document each activity. We noticed visual confirmation of the team's success when the number of videotapes needed to record the set-up went from four to three to two and eventually to one cassette.

Drills on Wheels

One $18,000 drilling machine at Bendix would have needed $12,000 in improvements in order to significantly reduce set-up time. The team could find no way to reduce set-up time using the "no-cost/low-cost" set-up reduction principles they had been taught in three days of training. Eventually, the team found a solution. It was to put the entire drilling machine on locking casters and to provide quick disconnects for all the air hoses, electrical conduits and ductwork connected to the machine.

The idea behind these changes was to make it possible to remove one drilling machine after the job was done and replace it with an entirely different drilling machine which was set-up for the next job. In other words, the entire set-up time was virtually eliminated by making all of it external. When Part #1 was running, Drilling Machine #2 was set up to run Part #2. When Part #1 was finished, Drill Machine #1 was disconnected and Drill Machine #2 was rolled and locked into place. What used to take 35 minutes and was fraught with quality problems now takes 5 minutes and runs trouble-free. This is an application of Stage Two of the Internal/External set-up method.

There are some that still say this isn't set-up reduction because the machine still takes the same amount of time to set up and that there has been no improvement. But, this is an example of true set-up reduction because there is now increased up-time available on this machine. In other words, Bendix' capacity problems were solved and Bendix was provided the flexibility to respond to automakers constant schedule changes.

MEREEN JOHNSON CORPORATION
Minneapolis, Minnesota

Mereen Johnson Corporation is a manufacturer of CNC (Computer Numerically Controlled) machine tools. They are a discrete, or job shop manufacturer, although they produce some items on a repetitive basis. Approximately 250 employees work at the company's two plants, about 300 miles apart. One plant is a union plant; the other is a non-union plant.

As part of the JIT implementation which Mereen Johnson requested, Jerry Claunch provided extensive education and training as the company started teams in the area of set-up reduction. The team consisted of a tool engineer, set-up person, operator, CNC programmer, clerical person, and supervisor. Their task was to look at the set-up of an indexing head on a CNC milling machine.

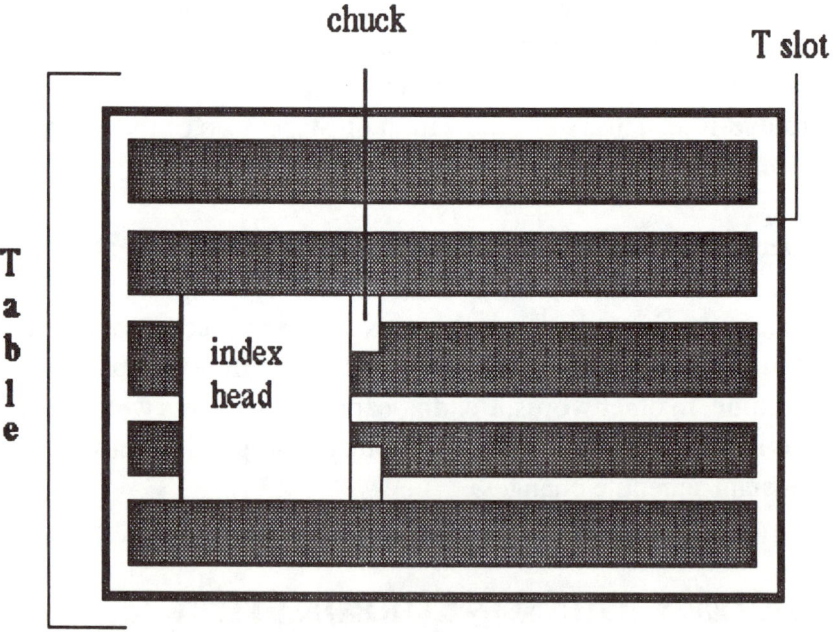

The two-hour set-up began with the placement of an index head on the table of the milling machine center. Prior to quick change, the indexing head would be placed on the work center two weeks out of the month in order to produce all the parts that they needed. Then, the indexing head would be taken off. This was done because there were some parts that required the full use of the table on the milling machine. The indexing head on the work center was then placed on the lower left hand corner of the milling machine table.

In a training session that we conducted, we viewed a videotape of the set-up person putting the indexing head on the milling machine. On the afternoon of the second day of training, the team began to brainstorm and came up with ideas of how they could reduce the set-up time on this indexing head. Using the videotape process described in Chapter 7 of this book, the team developed 10 to 15 ideas that they wanted to work on.

One of the people on the team, specifically the tool engineer, thought there was a possibility of adding a section onto the table of the milling machine. Then the set-up person could put the indexing head where it would be completely off the machine's table, but permanently mounted on its own table. The team decided to contact the manufacturer of the milling machine to see if this idea was feasible. They were concerned that the weight of the added table and the indexing head would prevent the milling machine from holding tolerances. They told the manufacturer what they were attempting and what restrictions there were for the automatic tool changer. The manufacturer of the milling machine studied the team's idea and advised them that there would be no problem to put the indexing head off to the side on its own securely fastened table.

Today, the indexing head is always on the machine, off to the side on a table, so that whenever they need it, it's available. Change-over time went from two hours to zero. That availability has allowed the people who program the parts to be manufactured on this milling machine. Previously, these people couldn't always program the parts for the indexing head because it wasn't always on the machine and because it took 2 hours to set up. They are now able to produce programs for all of the parts that they make. This has also improved quality.

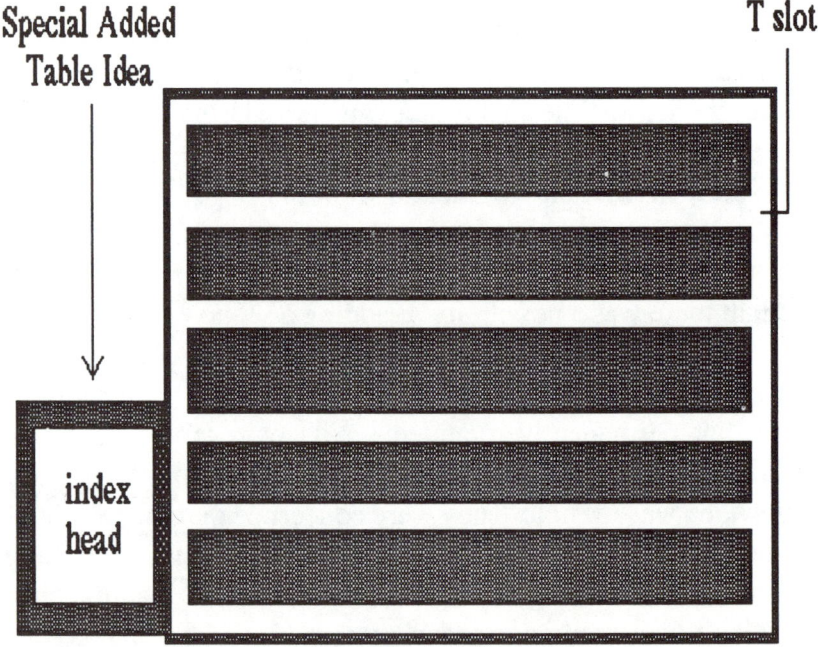

MEREEN JOHNSON CORPORATION
Webster, South Dakota

At the non-union plant, a set-up reduction team was working on a welding application. Their first task was to reduce the time it took for the weldment to set up for the bases of the CNC machines that they built. Equally as important was the need to address the quality of the parts which was in jeopardy due to the less than adequate set-up operations. This was because the parts were bowing out and losing squareness as they were set in place and welded.

The team designed a fixture which would allow them to quickly set the parts in the proper location and weld them so that the heat of the welding process didn't distort the weldment. The cost of that fixture was estimated by the team to be about $1,500 and they estimated the annual savings in scrap alone to be approximately $50,000 per year. The actual cost was lower because they were able to use some on-hand materials and their own labor within the facility to build the fixture. The savings were in excess of $50,000 in the first year alone.

Cost Benefit Analysis

Cost:
Labor
Materials
Machines

Total: $ 1,500

Benefits:
Labor
Materials
Machines

Total: $ 50,000

Approved: ☒ Yes ☐ No

The team that worked on this welding fixture was made up of shop floor employees, operators and supervisors off the factory floor.

At first, this team had a problem with estimating the cost and the benefit. We made it easy for them by initiating the following questions:

- **What's it going to cost in materials, machine time and labor to produce the fixture?**

- **What's it going to benefit you in labor, materials and machine time once it is completed?**

After we walked them through how to answer these questions, the team found that it was easy for them to calculate a cost/benefit analysis. It was gratifying, as we watched this team, to see that once they became comfortable with the process, they would have no problems doing it again in the future. In addition to getting the quick change and quality improvements, they also learned the process of cost justification.

MEREEN JOHNSON
Minneapolis, Minnesota

At Mereen Johnson, we had one very interesting problem because it wasn't with the setting up of the equipment they used to manufacture their product, but with the setting up of the equipment they sell to customers. We have noted before that companies that can improve the set-up time on the products they sell will be in a much stronger competitive position.

One of the problems that Mereen Johnson had during assembly of their product was the constant shimming and reworking of parts in order to assure a level line. Previously, they always used a long level so that they could level out the base and build it from there. Some of the employees felt that the set-up would go much faster and easier if they were able to level the equipment using a laser unit which would shoot a level beam. They were right. Now, when they set up the equipment they have sold, it goes very smoothly. In fact, many other problems went away, even the problems which used to occur when they installed the equipment at the customer's location since the equipment was set up in a perfectly level condition. This is an example of using technology, whether automation or robotics, judiciously.

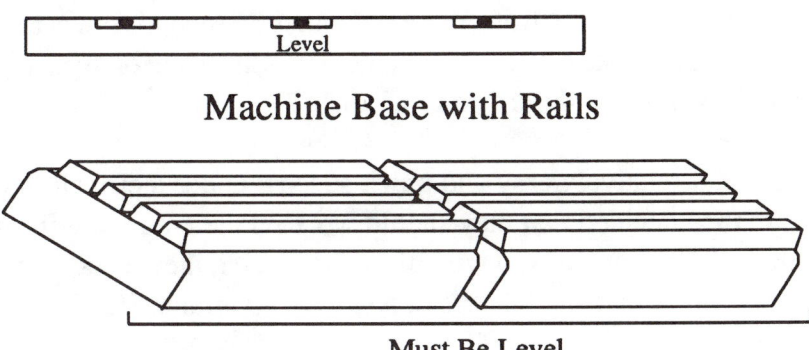

Machine Base with Rails

Must Be Level

Machine Base with Rails

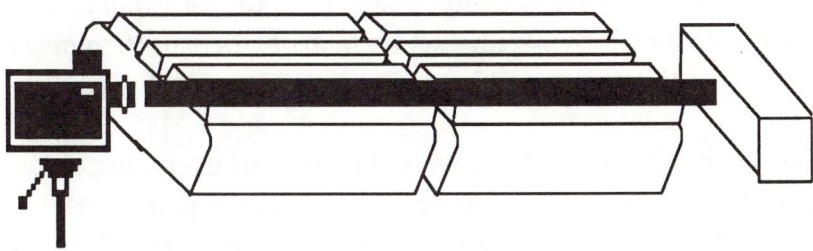

COSMAIR CORPORATION
Piscataway, New Jersey

Cosmair Corporation's Piscataway plant produces Lancôme products. At the Piscataway plant, the company produces mascara, creams and lipsticks. The set-up reduction team consisted of a supervisor, mechanic, set-up person, and two operators.

The team started set-up reduction on the part of the line where they fill bottles with the creams. Specifically, they worked on the capper operation where the cap is put on the bottle and were able to cut the set-up time from about 9 minutes 36 seconds down to 3 minutes 21 seconds. This improvement was the result of using the videotape process described in Chapter 7.

With that relatively easy and quick success under their belt, the team then decided that they should work on the entire line from one end to the other. And work they did. In fact, they reduced the line set-up time from 8 hours to less than 10 minutes!!!

Then, because they had greatly reduced changeover time on the line and had generated considerable dollar savings, the team decided to look at automation. Their analysis ended with the installation of three computer-controlled robots. These robots were programmed to handle whatever bottle of product they would run on the line. With a set-up tiem of less than 10 minutes, they were able to respond immediately to demand changes.

The changeover reductions were the result of instituting quick-change parts on their filling machines in order to eliminate the need for hand tools. They also bought duplicate parts, valves and

No Hand Tools

hoses so that they could clean them external to the changeover and so that they could be pre-set. Now, when these parts are brought out to the work center, they are ready to install immediately. The

NO Cleaing During Change Over

machine was operating most efficiently for the particular part, size, or bottle that they were filling. The team would go out to the line and document the setting so that they could duplicate that setting in the tool room. Before long, the team had eliminated the need for the operator to make adjustments to get the line to run smoothly.

GENERAL HOUSEWARES
Kewanee, Wisconsin

General Housewares is a manufacturer of cookware, primarily for the commercial industry which means the very large aluminum pots and pans that you would use in a restaurant rather than at home. They are a repetitive manufacturer with about 120 employees working in a union facility.

We began at General Housewares with the establishment of a cell to manufacture covers in a Just-In-Time (JIT) environment. After some training in JIT and set-up reduction, we instituted two set-up reduction teams to work on the process in the cell. This process began with a press which stamped the name on the cookware. The cover then went through a draw press which formed its overall shape. After this operation, it went through a turning lathe and finishing machines before passing through a wash station. Lastly, a spot welder affixed handles on the cover before the covers were packed.

This cell was set up in order to reduce the amount of time and the amount of labor that it took to get covers manufactured. The cell initially took 24 labor hours to produce 400 covers, or about 17

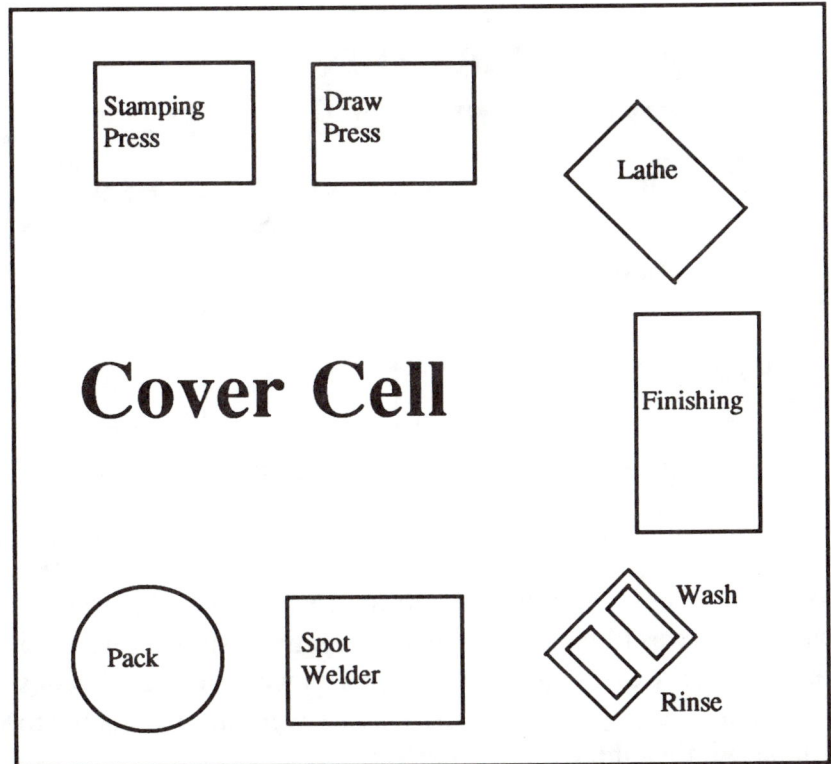

covers per hour. The old method of manufacturing covers only required 17 labor hours to produce 400 covers, but it took 25 days to get the covers through the facility from start to finish. But, with the cell arrangement, lead time was 6 hours, instead of 25 days. The chart on the next page demonstrates the improvements.

The washer was the bottleneck when the cell began. Before, the team looked at the problem, operators were basically washing by hand. The challenge put to the team was to come up with an easier, better, and quicker way to resolve the cleaning issue. Along with engineering, they designed an enclosed cleaning unit which used high-pressure spray. Now the covers just slide through.

SET-UP REDUCTION AT THE COVER MANUFACTURING CELL

AREA	OLD	NEW
Labor Hours	17	24
Rate	23.5/hr	17/hr
Lead Time	25 days	6 hrs

Work-in-process was eliminated because each cover, which started as a blank, was finished, wrapped and ready to ship out within a few minutes. Set-up time on the edge trim went from 24 minutes to 4 minutes. Set-up on the press to draw went from 1.5 hours to 1 hour within a three-month period of time.

Another goal of the team was to reclaim space. Work-in-process in their traditional manufacturing environment required 1,000 square feet for the covers alone. In comparison, the entire square footage of the new cell arrangement covered only 32 square feet. Work-in-process consisted of 6 covers—one between each work center in the cell, a pallet of blanks and a pallet of packaged covers.

Something happened at this plant which all companies should pay attention to. On one of our visits to General Housewares, the Operations Manager, Bob Orr (who was responsible for manufacturing), was somewhat depressed. We asked him why and he said, "Well, we're not seeing any results."

"How are the set-up teams doing?, " we wanted to know. He said he really didn't know. We discovered that the company had not been posting their measurements up on the wall for everyone to see. And that was unfortunate, because when we talked to the set-up reduction teams, we found out that both of them had cut set-up time by significant amounts. One set-up time had been cut to approximately 20% of its previous levels. The other team had cut set-up time down to 30% of previous levels.

Needless to say, the Operations Manger was quite excited when he received the good news and it was all he needed to get fired up again. This is an excellent example of the need to post measurements for all to see.

AGI CORPORATION
Chicago, Illinois

According to President Richard Block, AGI Corporation is a high volume, high quality printing company with about 150 employees. They are an example of a process manufacturing company. They have one plant in the Midwest and a sales office in New York City. We have been working with them on Statistical Process Control (SPC) using, for the most part, the approach outlined in Deming's fourteen steps. A natural step was for AGI to address the subject of make-ready reduction.

We started with two make-ready reduction teams on their printing press. The teams took videotapes. The tapes were about 9 1/2 hours long and required four different cameras because we had to watch four different people. There was the head pressman, the first pressman, a helper and a feeder. After completing the first vide-

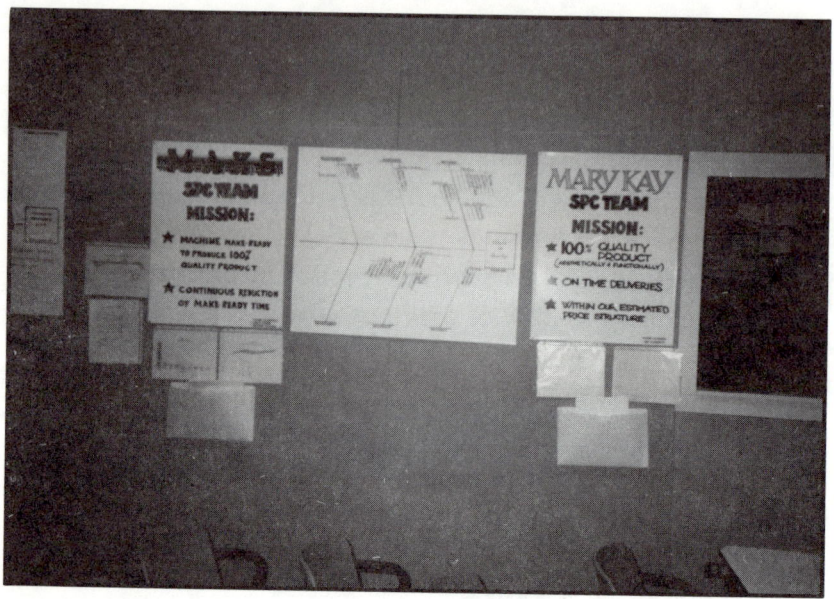

TEAM CHARTS, MEASUREMENTS AND FISHBONES

otape, we held a training session where we anticipated a lot of resistance since a printing press requires a lot of adjustment to run correctly. But, when we asked the four people previously identified if they thought they could cut the set-up time in half, they all said and believed that they could.

One of their first ideas was to contact the supplier and tell them what the team was doing. The supplier then asked what kind of roller they were using on the printing presses. It was a generic roller which is supposed to be good with either conventional or ultraviolet ink. One of the presses, however, never ran with conventional ink, only with ultraviolet ink. The supplier then told the team that he had some rollers that were designed to be used with ultraviolet ink and would absorb less ink, so that the wash-up time could be greatly shortened. The team asked the supplier to come in and demonstrate the product which he gladly did.

AGI then purchased enough rollers to completely outfit that particular press. The results were exactly what the supplier said they would be. The rollers were easier to clean up and took less time than the generic rollers. The team shortened the overall set-up time even further by putting some clamp pins on the photographic plates in order to locate them more accurately and quickly on the press. In other words, the team eliminated adjustment time.

The team developed other set-up reduction ideas which were implemented at AGI. One had to do with the fountain liners on the press. Press operators pour the ink into a fountain which coats the rollers. The rollers then ink the plate which prints the image on the paper. The team put liners in the fountain so that they would be able to remove them when a job was finished and eliminate the lengthy wash-up which they previously had to complete. They also came up with ink fountain catch pans so the ink would be recycled and not just run into a drum.

In addition, the team installed feed board wheels which allowed them to feed the board or paper they were using into the printing press with a higher degree of accuracy. They put quarter turn fasteners on the oscolation covers as well. They also purchased a new inking system which gives them a higher degree of accuracy and lets them know exactly how much ink is being placed on the product. As we have mentioned before, doing a cost/benefit analysis is one of the important functions of a team. The team at AGI did an excellent job of identifying and comparing their choices for a new inking system and ultimately justifying their decision. What follows is their actual report. We have eliminated brand names so as not to appear to favor one over the other.

Page 1

**AGI Justification by Make-Ready Team
for New Automated Ink Fountain System**

About four years ago, we installed a Company X automated ink fountain system on Press Number Nine. While this was a good step up from the standard ink system which had required the pressman to walk back and forth to the ink fountains every time a correction was necessary, it is being outdated by newer technology and is also in need of repair.

Since there are only two aftermarket ink fountain suppliers, Company X and Company Y, we have only three options.

> One — Repair the system we have.
> Two — Update to Company X new multi-
>   move system.
> Three — Update to Company Y new system.

Let's look at the possibilities.

Page 2

REPAIR PRESENT SYSTEM

Advantages

1. Cost — $15,000 approx. This is for segments only.

Disadvantages

1. Lack of speed — approx. 26 minutes
2. Continued sticking buttons causing runaways
3. Old motors and other parts — continued problems
4. Storage system doesn't work
5. Plate scanner inoperative
6. No preprogramming of next job
7. No remote sweep control
8. Higher waste
9. Slower make-ready time
10. Increased operator and customer frustration
11. Not compatible with scanning densitometer

Page 3

Company X Multi-Move System

Advantages

1. Faster than present system — 41 seconds vs. 26 minutes
2. Can preprogram new job while still running
3. Cost vs. Company X System
4. Updated storage system — reruns come back to color faster
5. All new parts
6. Eliminate runaways
7. Better engineering than present system or Company Y
8. Segmented fountain blade
9. Faster than present system to wash up
10. Speed is compatible to scanning densitometer
11. Known system — no learning curve
12. Present system worth something as trade-in

Disadvantages

1. Cost more than repair to present system

Page 4

Company Y System

Advantages

1. Easiest and faster to wash up
2. Speed vs. present system
3. Updated storage system — reruns come back to color faster
4. All new parts
5. Eliminate runaways
6. Speed is compatible to scanning densitometer
7. Able to preprogram next job

Disadvantages

1. Cost — most expensive option
2. Non-segmented blades
3. Unknown system — learning curve and motor burnouts
4. Engineering second to Company X
5. No trade-in on Press #9 or Press #8
6. Cost when necessary to update Press #8
7. Cannot use existing chips

Page 5

The team has seen both systems at the print show, had presentations from both companies, had an engineer examine both systems, called other users of the system and looked at the advantages/disadvantages of the three choices.

We feel to repair the present system would only be a stop-gap into which more money would have to be spent later and we would still have the same slow system holding us back.

We also agree that both cost and engineering have made the choice of updating to the Company Y system unacceptable.

Therefore, the team unanimously recommends the purchase of Company X new multi-move system. We would then have the speed and technology necessary to help reduce make-ready time and waste while providing more consistent product to our customers.

Respectfully Submitted,
Make-Ready Reduction Team

As you can undoubtedly see, teams made up of the real experts when given the proper training. We have never failed to see a well educated and trained team learn how to problem-solve or perform a cost/benefit analysis.

After all the changes above were made, the team cut the make-ready time from 9 1/2 hours to about 4 hours and 20 minutes. Their next task was to get the time even lower by cutting it in half again. The first action they performed was to videotape the set-up a second time because, at that point in time, the team was sure that the existing video no longer accurately depicted the set-up. They did make one change to the videotape process. Instead of doing one long tape, they taped only one segment of the make-ready at a time. Then they would brainstorm, implement their ideas and videotape another segment. This worked very well at AGI.

SECO PRODUCTS
A Middleby Company
Washington, Missouri

SECO Products is a major manufacturer of food service and healthcare equipment. Several years ago, SECO, then an IC Industries affiliate, embarked on an aggressive Just-In-Time (JIT) manufacturing program which included an emphasis on set-up reduction. The chosen pilot project was to attack long set-up/changeover times in the stainless steel and electrostatic coated shelving line. These products are used in both dry and refrigerated storage of food products.

According to Gene Kozemski, SECO's Operations Manager, the major reasons for selecting the shelving line as the pilot project were:

- **Excessive inventory levels.**

- **Inability to respond to customer "rush" orders.**

- **Quality problems associated with large lot sizes and/or unplanned changeovers.**

Utilizing the team approach and relying on the skill and experience of set-up people and operators, the following innovative solutions were developed:

- Pinned, positive stops for accurate width and length settings on the automatic forming presses.

- Motorized lead screw adjustments for speed and accuracy.

- Modifications in welding processes, producing higher quality/less rejections and faster first "good" piece production from the automatic corner welders.

- Enhancements to the cut to length/blanking line, centering on positive locator pins.

- "Partnership" with the steel supplier to guarantee delivery of correct width tolerances on time, every time, spearheaded by Mike Ebert, Purchasing Manager.

These changes have brought about significant benefits, according to Mr. Kozemski. Lot sizes have been reduced from an eight weeks (forecast) supply to building every shelf (part number) every week while dovetailing with incoming orders. SECO has had an overall inventory reduction of $500,000, or 60 percent, with a bottom line impact of approximately $160,000. Customer on-time delivery performance has improved by 25 percent as has the company's responsiveness to spikes in customer demand. Quality has also been greatly enhanced because of smaller lot sizes and less rejects and reworks. Most importantly, all of these results were achieved on a low-cost/no-cost basis and they have provided a baseline from which to measure continuous improvement at SECO Products.

CHAPTER THIRTEEN

GENERAL FOODS
A CASE STUDY

We have done extensive work with General Foods and believe their accomplishments deserve a separate chapter. We would also like to express our sincere thanks to Plant Manger Dick Chalfant, Human Resource Manager Sam Nichols and Logistic Manager and Steering Committee Chairman Yone Dewberry for their support throughout the program that still continues to this day. Needless to say, this is the type of commitment and drive that more companies need to prosper, even survive, in the 1990s and beyond. Special thanks and admiration also are due to the many men and women who worked diligently to reduce set-up times and who never ceased to amaze us with their creativity and perseverance. Our hats are off to all.

GENERAL FOODS
Dover, Delaware

In the Baker's Chocolate Dry Stock area at General Foods, the employees take chocolate that's been melted, mixed and blended and mill it until it becomes very fine shavings, or dry stock. The product is used extensively by candy and cookie manufacturers.

In the dry stock area, they cooled it down even further to make sure that it didn't clump when packaged. The chocolate is conveyed to the dry stock processing area which consists of a CO_2 chamber. Once cooled, the product then runs through a screen which separates the chocolate. After the chocolate is packaged, it is stored in a conditioned warehouse to prevent future clumping of the product.

The first problem the team had in addressing set-up reduction was that the company hadn't eliminated all the problems that they had with the initial installation of the machine. We recommended that they address these issues first before starting set-up reduction. This was a new and innovative suggestion at the plant. The normal course of action was to turn such problems over to Manufacturing. We did not start set-up reduction until the operators were satisfied that the equipment was operating as intended.

Once the set-up reduction team started, they came up with a number of areas that needed to be enhanced. One idea was as simple as installing a floor drain to help with clean-up during changeovers. They were required, between different kinds of product such as chocolate and caramel, to completely wash down the equipment. Initially, there was no drain at all in the area where they washed down this equipment. So all the water and product would gather on the floor and the operators would have to squeegee the dirty water up with mops, haul the waste over to a drain, which was a football field away, and dump it out. It literally took hours.

Wash Down Requires a Floor Drain in the Immediate Area

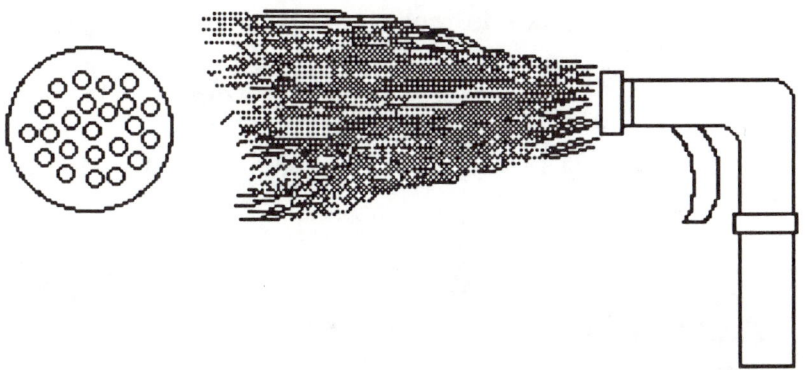

After observing the changeover, the team simply asked, "Why don't we put a drain in there?" The team, which consisted of operators who did their own changeovers, some engineers and a manager, also had some research people on the team simply because we wanted them to understand the whole manufacturing of dry stock. One research person who was well-respected in the organization, made a comment about the floor drain which took us back at first. "If I could just interrupt the team here a minute," he said. "When we put this floor drain in, let's put it in the lowest part of the floor this time."

Had that come from somebody else, it would have been a wise crack. But Matt Wyant, the research person who made the statement, had been around the plant for a number of years.

"I've seen them put drains at the highest points," he told the team. "You still have to squeegee the waste water." This time, the set-up team put a white chalk mark exactly where the floor drain needed to be.

One of the problems they had with changeovers was the excessive amount of time it took to replace the filter bags that kept the

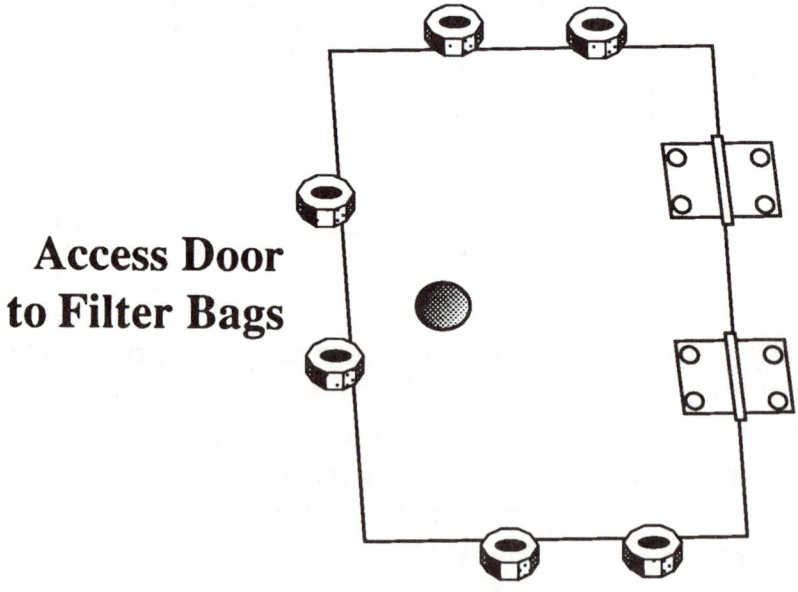

**Access Door
to Filter Bags**

chocolate dusting from settling all over the place. Since a wrench was needed to open the cabinet to change these bags, the operators were required to call one of the trades, the maintenance department, to open the covers and remove the bags. At times, it took approximately 6 hours for them to finally get a maintenance person over to change the bags so they could start up. It was totally wasted time.

We decided at that time to start a task force that would go to every location in the plant, approximately 25-30, where these filter systems were in use and turn the replacement of the filter bags into quick-change operation. The task force's goal is to perform the changeover so that no hand tools are required and so that the changeover can be done in minutes by the operators or the set-up people. At the time of publication, this team which consisted of two engineers, a maintenance person and a supervisor, were identifying every filter location within the plant so that they could begin set-up reduction on all of them. This is an excellent example of why companies need to clone. If something is happening in one area, you can safely assume it's going to happen in other areas where they have the same application.

GENERAL FOODS
Jell-OManufacturing
Dover, Delaware

One of the problems that General Foods had in the Jell-O manufacturing area was getting the lines properly cleaned when they went to three production shifts. Doing changeovers and getting the lines cleaned became an enormous problem. They have eight processing lines which take the powdered gelatin mix and drop it from one floor to the next. Then it goes down into a machine that dispenses 3 ounces of product into a pouch which is sealed and put into a box that you purchase at the store as Jell-O. Each line is approximately 50 feet long and within 15 feet of each other.

To change over one line, the set-up people have to clean it with some liquid. Water, of course, caused rusting if they did not dry it quickly enough. To overcome this problem, they preferred to use compressed air. The only problem with compressed air is that it is very dangerous if you're close to someone when using it. OSHA rules said that they weren't supposed to use any more than 30 pounds of pressure. But, 30 pounds didn't adequately clean the clamps, rollers and gears which get caked with the sugar and gelatin as it is packaged. The set-up reduction team's solution was to put some tarps onto some movable frames. They could then move the frames between the other line and clean them with either compressed air or water so as not to disturb the other lines around them that were running.

Another idea that the set-up reduction team implemented occurred in the area called pouch formation. The equipment they use to form the pouches is circular. It comes around and grabs the paper pouch after it has been sealed on three sides and squeezes it so that the top opens up. This allows a pouch to be formed so that the product can be dropped in. Before implementing the new idea, much of the product would be scattered around the area, on the pouches and on the equipment. The team decided to install a number of air lines which would blow air at different angles in order to blow off any excess product every time the equipment cycled around. They formed a curtain of air pressure which kept

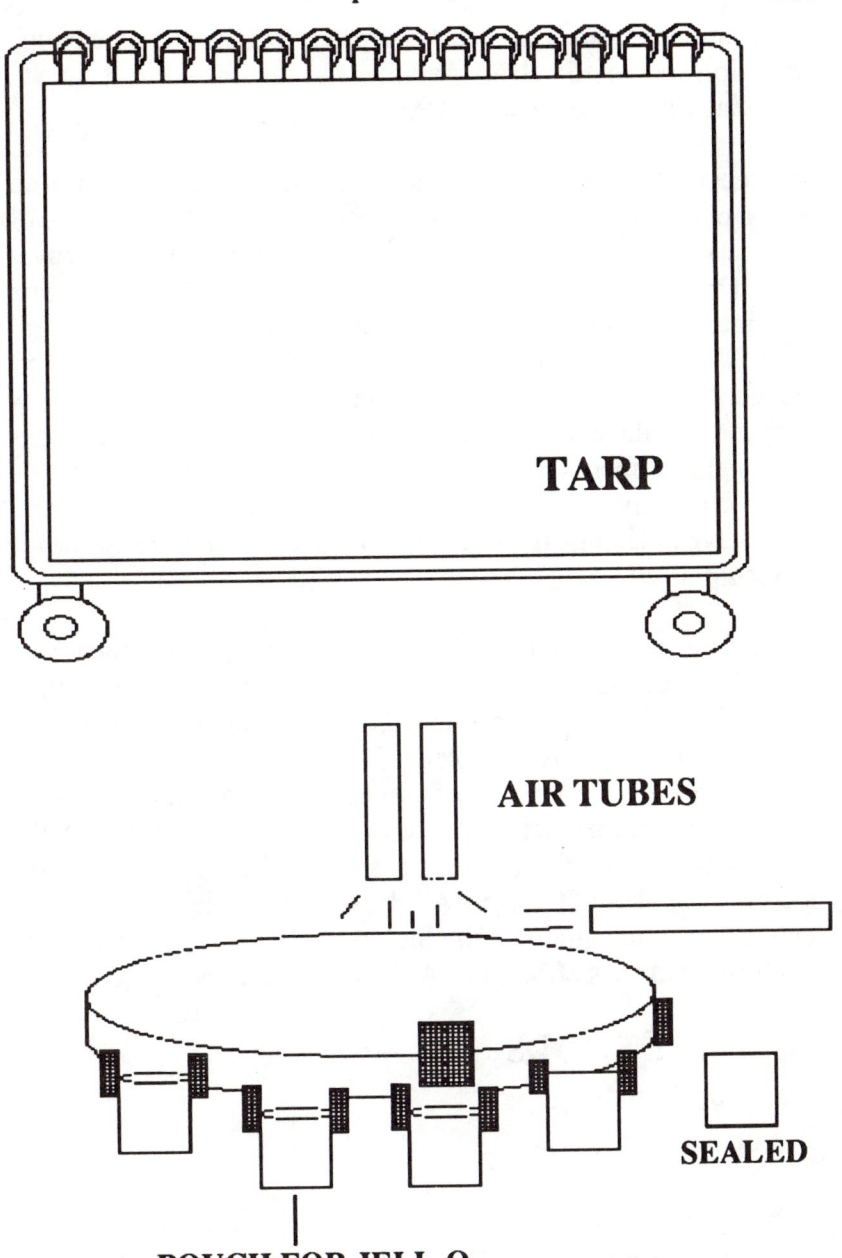

TARP

AIR TUBES

SEALED

POUCH FOR JELL-O

the equipment clean. The results were very good. It kept the pouch formation area totally clean at all times so that they didn't have to come back periodically and clean it.

One recent development at General Foods was the decision to close a plant and move the volume to the Dover plant. Because of that decision, there was additional equipment moved to the Dover plant. One particular piece was a very high volume, long run machine. The team decided to take advantage of this new equipment. They determined what flavors (strawberry and cherry) needed high volumes and dedicated the lines with the new equipment to those flavors so that they never had to do a changeover on those lines. This is in keeping with the direction we give to any company. If you can dedicate a line to one product and never have to change it over, then do it because *the best set-up is no set-up at all.*

One of the teams that we facilitated in the Jell-O plant was working on the Jell-O Pudding line. The problem was that they didn't always have consistency from one changeover person to another on how to solve problems. They also didn't have consistency with the operators. The team developed a troubleshooting guide for the machines. It identified what the trouble might be, the possible causes and the action they should take. They now have a document of about 20 pages. All the set-up people and operators regularly use this guide on the line to change over, maintain and run the lines at peak efficiency. A sample appears on the next page.

GENERAL FOODS
Stovetop Stuffing
Dover, Delaware

Probably one of the best examples of set-up and changeover reduction is at the General Foods plant which produces Stovetop

TROUBLE-SHOOTING GUIDE

Trouble	Possible Cause	Action
No product	• Slide gate closed	• Put slide gate on auto
	• Sifter off	• Turn sifter on
	• Sifter plugged	• Open and clean sifter
	• Feed screw not working a) Is jam switch lit? b) Does the screw turn in hand?	a) If yes, clear jam b) If yes, level probe not working. Call Instrument Shop. If no, jam switch not actuated. Call electrician.
	• Sifter sock is too long	• Remove clamps, shorten sock
Product not feeding from Perry wheel	• DOSE switch off • Air pressure too low	• Turn to DOSE • Increase air to proper regulation

Stuffing. They started with two set-up reduction teams. One basically dealt with the box that they put the product into and the changes they make when they go from one box size to another. The other changeover team dealt with what they called a flavor-to-flavor changeover. (The box size didn't change, just the product in the box.)

First, let's look at how the improvements made in the flavor-to-flavor changeover helped the company. As we discuss this example, remember that, when the line was running a certain size box, all the different flavors of stovetop stuffing — chicken, pork, turkey, etc. — would be run. The team began the project by compiling a complete checklist of all the steps that were involved during a flavor-to-flavor changeover.

CHECKLIST OF STEPS
FLAVOR-TO-FLAVOR

- **Draw off excess product**
  - **Bread crumbs**
  - **Spices**
  - **Vegetables**
- **Clean out bins**
- **Clean out flow tubes**

They also compiled information about production runs by installing a scheduling board out where the production scheduler could write down what quantity they were going to run for the week. Then, they put counters on the line so that at the beginning of the shift you could look at how many you were supposed to run and how many had been run, and know exactly how many were left to be run.

Next, they determined how many cases of product they could fill with 100 pounds of spice. By knowing this, the team would know when to stop mixing more spice. In other words, if 100 pounds of spice filled 100 cases and if the line had 50 pounds of spice left and only 20 more case to fill, then the operators would know not to mix any more spice. To aid in this area, the team also installed some

100 LBS. OF SPICE = "X" CASES	
Chicken	
Pork	
Beef	
Etc.	
Etc.	

telephones. The people that mixed the spices were on the level above the people that packaged it and they had no way of talking to each other. They installed some closed circuit phones so that all they did was pick up the phone below, and someone upstairs would answer it.

The team then determined that since they knew when the change-over was coming, now that they had a schedule board and counters, they could make sure that the bins weren't kept full of product, like celery and carrots, when a changeover was imminent. Also, each operator would have his or her own bin which the person one level above would keep full. Armed with information about how many more cases needed to be filled and a telephone with which to communicate with the person on the floor above, the operators were able to let the bin run lower. Therefore, when the changeover came, the bin wasn't full and they didn't have to draw the product off.

There are heater bars on the line which used to take the pouch material (basically a roll of paper), fold it over and seal it up. The heater bars are two separate units and one of the team members came up with the idea of making it one single unit. The team asked

Maintenance to construct the new single unit, but it never got done. Finally, this team member decided out of frustration one Saturday to make the new heater bars himself. He got a grievance filed against him and they had to pay the maintenance people four hours of overtime which they said that they lost because the team member made the new heater bars himself. The money spent was well worth it. The new heating and sealing unit made a significant contribution toward reducing set-up time since it eliminated a great deal of adjustment.

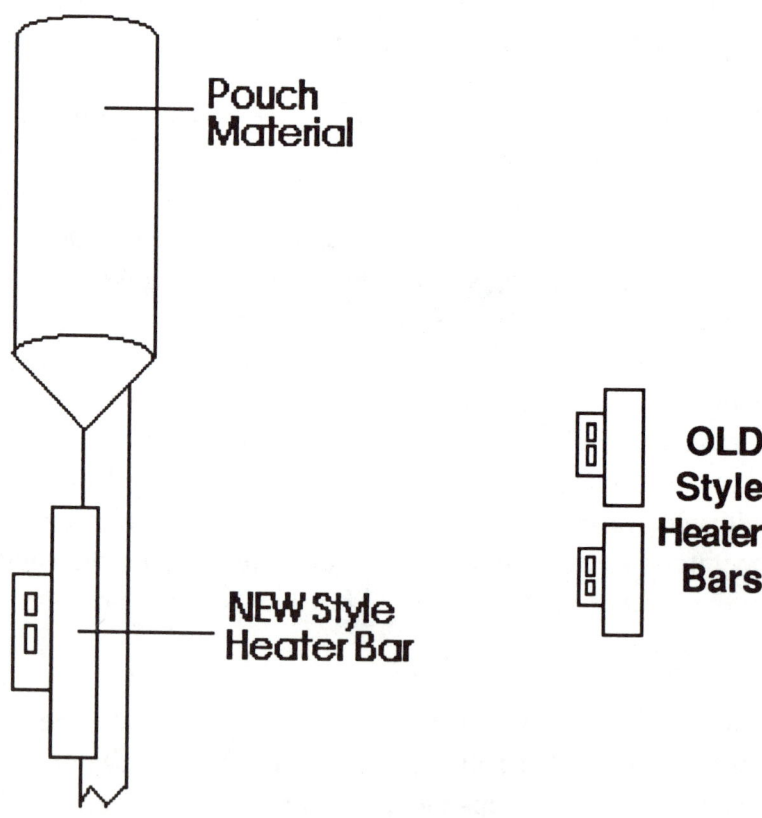

At this particular location, the employee involvement team came up with a totally new layout for the company. General Foods Corporate decided to implement cellular technology and manufacture similar products together. Since Stovetop was in the meals division, they decided they would move all the meals product to the same location in the plant. It was going to cost them about $5 million dollars.

When the team heard about this move, they said, "Why would you spend $5 million just to move it? Why don't you let us do a new layout that would allow you to bring the bread crumbs, spices and vegetables in one door so that it can be processed and sent out another door? Why don't you let us use the $5 million to make the department more efficient and to eliminate waste?"

The corporate office agreed and gave the team $2.7 million. The team went and asked Engineering to design three layouts which would support a better process flow. They actually trained Engineering in the principles of continuous improvement in order to reach their goal of never having material stop in the flow. During the designing of the new department layout, the team reviewed the layout five or six times to make improvements. By the time the layout was completed, there was no problem getting the employees to accept it since they were actively involved in its development. The results were immediate as well—reductions in cost and set-up in addition to saving $2.3 million out of the $5 million originally allocated.

In problem-solving with a set-up reduction team, one of the problems we encountered was the need for more training in order to reduce set-up times even further. So the team went to work

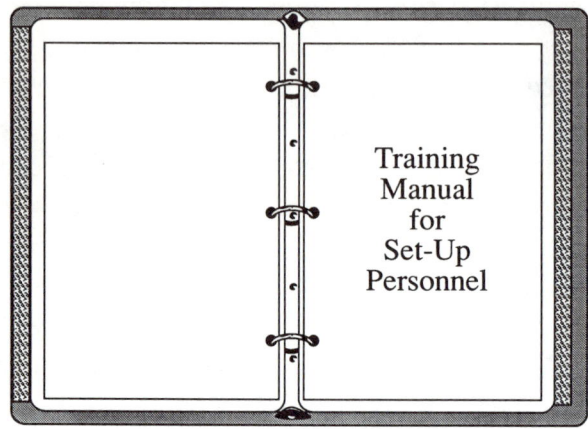

Training
Manual
for
Set-Up
Personnel

developing a complete training program and schedule so that all set-up people were trained to do changeovers the same way. Then the team found that even the six supposedly identical machines which dropped the product into pouches were hindering problem-solving because none of the machines was the same. They were all made by the same manufacturer and had the same model number, but they had been revamped many times over the years. Certain

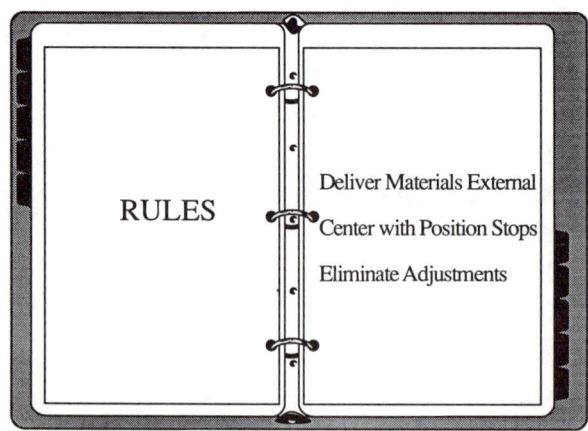

RULES

Deliver Materials External

Center with Position Stops

Eliminate Adjustments

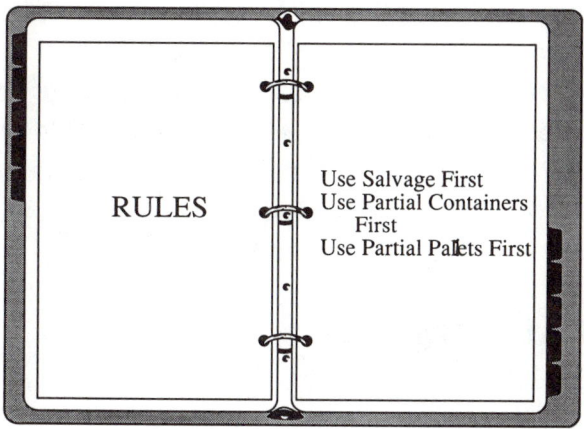

things done to some machines weren't done to all of them. Some, in fact, had dials which you would turn to the right in order to increase the amount of product that was produced, while on the other machines you had to turn it to the left. It was impossible for an operator to go to any machine and start running it, so the team began a program to refurbish, standardize and computerize all the machines.

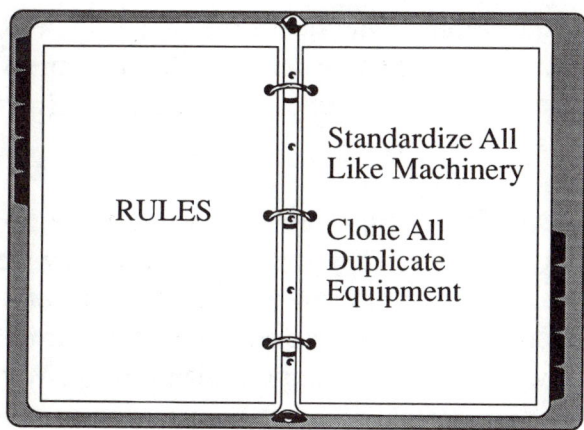

Another problem the set-up reduction team successfully solved was what to do with any salvage left over at the end of a run. In the past, they never made an attempt to use the salvage first, so the team decided that they could solve the salvage problem and reduce inventory at the same time. Today, the first thing a set-up person does when they set up is fill the hoppers with any salvage that was left over from a previous run.

GENERAL FOODS
Dover, Delaware

The last words in this chapter have to do with commitment and how to get people on the side of set-up reduction. As mentioned, we started a team at Baker's Chocolate in the cocoa processing area. At a training session for the people in this area, they told us that they would believe us when we said we were committed to the elimination of waste if we got the #1 press fixed so that it would stop leaking.

On this equipment, the operator would put chocolate into the press in order to squeeze the butter out of the chocolate which would then separate into cocoa powder. Well, when press #1 was squeezing the chocolate, the butter was leaking out of all the hoses and making a complete mess.

When the team first brought up this problem, we hoped they weren't being negative. They weren't. In fact, they were being very honest. The employees saw a drastic example of waste that no one was addressing. If we were really committed to eliminating waste, they wanted to see action on this problem. We then got together with the plant manager and the maintenance manager and got their commitment to fix the press.

Once the press was fixed, it was easy to get the team to do set-up reduction and other waste elimination because we had demonstrated that we were committed to it. Because of this example and many others, we encourage companies contemplating set-up reduction or any kind of continuous improvement to listen to employees. We ought to listen to them and fix the problems that they see day after day and prove to them that we're getting ready now to meet the future.

CHAPTER FOURTEEN

WHAT'S NEXT?
THE FUTURE WE'VE FUNDED

A look to our past reveals American manufacturers as world leaders because they never rested on their laurels. That American spirit which drove people across this continent was the same spirit which created an industrial might the world has never known. That spirit is still with us, but there is a need to focus (and stay focused) on both our problems and their solutions. This is not the time for companies to jump from one concept to another. This is not the time to be satisfied with the considerable progress we have made to meet the global challenge. Any good marathoner will tell you that the critical point in a race is that moment when an extra effort is required. This is the point where the runner has to pick up the pace. Sometimes it's not the body which prevents the runner from going faster, but his or her mind-set.

Some marathoners report that, at this point in the race, their mind tries to convince the runner that he or she has done a good job already. "You can coast to victory," the mind seems to be saying.

The same thoughts, of course, are going on in the mind of the marathoner who is fifty yards behind the leader. But, instead of settling for second, this runner decides to dig deeper, to use the power of his mind to will his body to greater performances. We have all seen the results of such thinking many times — the leader is passed on the final lap in the stadium.

We don't want to see American companies passed by the competition. But we also know, as we gaze into the future, that we will get passed if we don't start addressing set-up reduction *today*!

THE STAGE IS SET

The curtain is coming up on a new stage in manufacturing. This stage is set with a new design which coordinates all the operations of a company. We call this new, company-wide philosophy for management the Total Business Concept (TBC). The principal aims of TBC are to eliminate waste and to use the generated savings to fund future improvements.

No company should start to play a role on this new stage without doing what every theater professional knows is essential. The curtain never goes up until the stage is "pre-set," that is, all the walls, the furniture, the props, the doors, the murder weapons, or whatever are in their proper places. An actor who needs to kill an intruder in the second scene must expect to find the gun in the desk drawer. If she doesn't because somebody forgot to "pre-set" the gun, she is going to look ridiculous in front of an entire theater filled with people. Furthermore, the production of a story which is supposed to entertain people will be disrupted and they will leave talking about the poor quality of the play.

In these respects, the production of a play is not much different than the production of CNC equipment or bottled water. If the company fails to "pre-set," there will be unhappy customers. Manufacturers, indeed all companies, need to address the components of TBC. There are some roles which companies will need to learn and rehearse. Set-up reduction is one of them and it dovetails nicely with all the other parts of the new stage design which we will discuss next. This is what the future will look like. This is what we need to do in order to set up our companies for that future.

WHAT WE NEED TO DO

The philosophy of TBC is about bringing cohesiveness, unity and integration into a company. In general, it has these characteristics:

1. On-line, real-time information about both internal and external operations. Current information coupled with a documented past is extremely useful information.

2. Accurate information. We all know that a small mistake compounds over time. Unlike

interest on your personal investments, this is
not favorable. The surveyor who makes a
mistake of one degree can cost you many
valuable acres of land.

3. No waste present in operations. Waste,
    today, is too often accepted as a given and
    absorbed into overhead costs. This is truly a
    reactive way of thinking and must change as
    we compete in a world market. Remember:
    set-up is waste.

4. Comparison of actual performance to the
    stated plan. Observing this variance is
    instrumental in making new plans which
    take corrective action. Those who don't
    learn from the mistakes of the past are
    doomed to repeat them.

CREATE TRUE PARTNERSHIPS

TBC also means the creation of true partnerships with suppliers to
reduce set-up and lower lot sizes. First, there needs to be a clear
commitment by management at all levels of both organizations.
Second, there must be *visible/measurable* set-up reduction programs in both companies. These types of programs mean that
achieved results are plotted against the objectives and goals to
track performance of the program. Third, both companies need to
embrace a *zero-defect* philosophy which states "do it right the first
time" and that a company does not accept continued rejects at any
point in the process. Fourth, both companies must comply to

lower lot sizes and *on-time delivery,* the arrival of material when it is required and not before or after. The objective is to use material as soon as it hits the receiving dock (Ship-To-Stock) and eventually to have material shipped directly to the line (Ship-To-WIP).

MEET CUSTOMER EXPECTATIONS

The future will also require companies which are flexible enough to meet customer expectations. If expectations change, then companies need to change their products, machines and factories which produce. Besides meeting the requirements set forth by the specifications, conformance to requirements also means providing good answers to the following questions:

• Does the product relate to quick changeover?
• Does the product meet customer needs?
• Does it meet Engineering specifications?
• Does it meet manufacturing process requirements?
• Is the product producible?
• Does the product meet test requirements?

We believe that products must meet customer requirements. The problem with American manufacturers is that they often fail to determine what is needed or wanted by their customers. A good example is custom corrugated cartons. We were involved in a situation in which a company using custom cartons could fit their product into standard cartons simply by adjusting one dimension. They had difficulty changing the dimension because it wasn't in the specifications and had to be sent to Engineering Change Control. They then have to see whether the change makes any difference to their customers. In many cases, the change made no difference and they were able to lower the total cost with no set-up required.

IMPROVE DELIVERY PERFORMANCE

The future will require us to measure on-time delivery in two ways — in terms of dollars and days. This measurement addresses the company's performance to the customer as well as the receipt of materials from the supplier and internal processes. Concerning our performance to the customer, we must measure the actual shipment date to the scheduled and/or requested date. Delivery performance as it relates to supplier and internal processes is measured by comparing actual receipt date to the confirmed scheduled delivery date. Set-up reduction improves delivery performance by improving flexibility.

IMPROVE QUALITY

In Deming's approach to quality improvement, he advises companies to "make maximum use of statistical knowledge and talent." Why? Because techniques like SPC (Statistical Process Control) are the manufacturing embodiment of the old saying that an ounce of prevention is worth a pound of cure. SPC lets us know when machines are about to produce a bad part before they actually do. This is because statistics allows us to note trends in variances. Once we have noticed assignable variances, we are then able to make changes which insure control over the process. These factors are important in this area of set-up reduction and preventive maintenance because it is difficult to have process capability on a machine which is constantly in need of repair or of being overhauled.

REDUCE INVENTORY

Since the intent of TBC is to get the right material to the right place at the right time so that every procedure or operation adds value to the product, it is clear that you should want to lower lot sizes through a set-up reduction program. This will result in less material in the plant since it does not sit in storage or queues adding carrying costs to your bottom line.

Over half of lead time is taken up by queues. We can greatly reduce queue time by shipping directly to the line and even eliminate queues outright in a true TBC environment. Couple queue reduction with set-up reduction and you can readily see that we don't have to accept lead times as unchangeable. Purchasing, by monitoring progress on set-up and queue reduction, plays a large role in shortening lead times. Shorter lead times lead to a higher inventory turnover rate and a greater return on assets.

In the book, **MADE IN AMERICA:** *The Total Business Concept*, Peter L. Grieco, Jr and Michael W. Gozzo noted that the measurement of inventory turns is perhaps the single best method for determining the progress you are making toward surviving in the future. We can increase inventory turns by planning for only as much material as a work station needs to make one unit of product once we have minimized set-up time.

Most companies today are struggling to achieve three inventory turns a year. This means they carry four months of inventory. We have worked with companies that have raised the level to 14 turns, 26 turns, 36 turns, even 42 turns a year. Obviously, these companies have been able to coordinate many of the variables which constitute TBC through the set-up reduction process.

DATA ACCURACY
AND PAPERWORK REDUCTION

These two are so intertwined in set-up reduction in office areas that we present them as two sides of the same opportunity. All of the different company operations and departments cannot coordinate their activities until there is a common base that is measured and monitored. By simply monitoring paperwork and then reducing process time, any company will automatically improve accuracy.

Accuracy is what we call an "up-front" consideration. There are two reasons for this. One, we exist in a manufacturing environment where quick change is a necessity. Two, we simply can't forecast, plan, schedule or produce without the most basic of raw materials — accurate information.

CUT TRANSPORTATION COSTS

We also need to look more closely at how set-up reduction in the transportation area ties into the TBC concept. The point, obviously is to reduce set-up costs and find the most economical means of transportation. One client, for example, has installed bar coding equipment at the loading ramp. Every piece loaded into a truck is scanned so that all manual entry and shipping papers have been eliminated. Here are some other questions we should be asking ourselves:

---

1. What are the set-up procedures in receiving?
2. What is the cost of detrashing and packing?
3. What percentage of delivered freight requires some sort of set-up?

WHAT ARE THE BENEFITS OF SET-UP REDUCTION?

Set-up reduction is one part of a panoply of activities which will prepare your company for the future. The benefits which can be derived from a set-up reduction program inside of a TBC environment will not only prepare your company for the future, but will help you to fund that future. The benefits below can make any Continuous Improvement Process self-funding. Let us briefly list and explain some of the direct benefits:

- Lower cost of purchased parts — a result of better relations with suppliers, lower inventory costs, better coordination between purchasing and design, production and planning.

- Greatly improved quality — actual cost of material is only one item and not as important an item as the delivery of zero-defect material which will flow continuously through your plant.

- Better design and producibility — new products are not produced behind closed doors and then thrown over walls to unprepared and sometimes obstinate production departments. Design now works with purchasing, production, marketing and even shop floor people to make designs that work and that are far cheaper to produce.

- Improved administrative efficiency — as paperwork diminishes and people truly communicate and work together, administrative coordination develops naturally.

- Increased productivity — in terms of the shop floor, better flow of material, faster set-up and lead times, and elimination of wasted time, machines and operations. Productivity is not necessarily the same as automation.

As for indirect benefits, who can say, for example, at exactly what point a company adopting set-up reduction has an earlier and sharper visibility into its operations? When a company changes from being reactive to proactive? When it becomes mentally receptive to the Total Business Concept? When it will be ready to face the future?

FUNDING THE FUTURE

What role will set-up reduction play in funding your company's future? A very large role. For instance, with reduced inventories, companies will be able to:

- Increase capital turnover.
- Free up storage space for manufacturing use.
- Reduce stock-handling operations.
- Perform mixed production.
- Ship on time, 100 percent of the time.

Machine work rates will also improve and productive capacity will expand as we saw with Bendix in a previous chapter. As set-ups become quicker and easier, the number of set-up errors will disappear and consequently the number of defective goods diminishes. Also, the need for special set-up skills will be eliminated. Both safety and tool management improve as well. In short, set-up reduction can shorten production times to the point where changes in demand can be responded to immediately. This will be necessary for survival in the future.

One practice we would like to see avoided is set-up reduction programs dying out because Corporate stops funding the program. The above benefits should more than pay for any program. As long as companies get set-up reduction and then lot size reduction, they will find their inventory levels decreasing. The savings which can be derived from paying far less carrying costs on inventory will fund the program. We have seen it happen many, many times. We have seen many companies who were able to put savings against the bottom line as well.

WHERE TO FROM HERE?

We have brought you this far. You know the challenge is to keep your company competitive in domestic and international markets. After reading this book, you have the means to meet that challenge. If you have learned anything from this book, you should have learned that the job never stops. You must make a continuous improvement effort to achieve excellence and World Class Status.

We believe that set-up reduction supports the movement toward the focus factory by simplifying production processes and eliminating waste on the factory floor. Set-up reduction supports key design criteria for Computer Integrated Manufacturing (CIM). Our belief is that the business philosophy we have discussed throughout this book will now allow you to selectively automate key production facilities and move in the direction of total factory automation and integration. That movement is the movement toward CIM.

Set-up reduction is a highly visible area which can act as a great motivator to the implementation of other JIT practices. For example, we have a client who was able to reduce one set-up time from 35 minutes to 9 seconds. Broadcasting that reduction around the plant only served to make people want to reduce the set-up times at their work centers by similar percentages.

It is quite evident that reduced set-up times increase productivity and subsequently lower inventory levels. Another equally valid result is the ability now for production lines to be much more flexible and to reduce lot sizes. This, in turn, allows you to come closer and closer to building products based on actual demand without storing excess inventory.

CONCLUSION

We are confident about the future. We advise all of you to take the steps outlined in this book and apply them throughout your companies, not only on your factory floors. The principles can be applied to any set-up, operation or administrative task.

We have observed many examples of reducing set-up times and have found that a properly trained team is essential for success. They must be dedicated. At one client, we witnessed an excellent example of a team which is living and breathing set-up reduction. This company has a paging system for key personnel to report to work centers being set up. In the past, somebody would say the following over the system:

"John Smith, please come to work center #9."

Now that they are thinking set-up reduction, they say:

"John Smith, please come to work center #9 and bring the adjustment wrench."

This is the attitude we think companies must have. Remember: Time is money and a minute saved is dollars earned. This is how we can turn "sense" into dollars.

BIBLIOGRAPHY

HANDBOOK OF PRODUCT DESIGN FOR MANUFAC-TURING, James G. Bralla, Editor in Chief, McGraw-Hill Book Company, New York, NY.

Peter L. Grieco, Jr., Michael W. Gozzo, Jerry W. Claunch, **JUST-IN-TIME PURCHASING:** *In Pursuit of Excellence*, PT Publications, Inc., Palm Beach Gardens, FL.

Peter L. Grieco, Jr., Michael W. Gozzo, Jerry W. Claunch, **SUPPLIER CERTIFICATION:** *Achieving Excellence*, PT Publications, Inc., Palm Beach Gardens, FL.

302

Peter L. Grieco, Jr., Michael W. Gozzo, C.J. (Chip) Long, **BEHIND BARS:** *Bar Coding Principles and Applications*, PT Publications, Inc., Palm Beach Gardens, FL.

Peter L. Grieco, Jr., Michael W. Gozzo, **MADE IN AMERICA:** *The Total Business Concept*, PT Publications, Inc., Palm Beach Gardens, FL.

Shigeo Shingo, **STUDY OF TOYOTA PRODUCTION SYSTEM from Industrial Engineering Viewpoint**, Japan Management Association, Tokyo, Japan.

H. Thomas Johnson, Robert S. Kaplan, **RELEVANCE LOST:** *The Rise and Fall of Management Accounting*, Harvard Business School Press, Boston, MA.

Tom Peters, **THRIVING ON CHAOS:** *Handbook for a Management Revolution*, Knopf, New York, NY.

Armand V. Feigenbaum, **TOTAL QUALITY CONTROL**, McGraw-Hill Book Co., New York, NY.

PRODUCTION AND INVENTORY MANAGEMENT REVIEW and APICS NEWS, Raymond G. Feldman, Editor; Richard D'Alessandro, Publisher; Hollywood, FL.

MODERN MACHINE SHOP, Ken M. Gettelman, Editor, Gardner Publications Inc., Cincinnati, OH.

PURCHASING MAGAZINE, James P. Morgan, Editor, John F. O'Connor, Publisher, Cahners Publishing Co., Newton, MA.

W. Edwards Deming, OUT OF THE CRISIS, MIT Center for Advanced Engineering Study, Cambridge, MA.

HARVARD BUSINESS REVIEW, Theodore Levitt, Editor; James A. McGowan, Publisher; Boston, MA.

Thomas J. Peters, Robert H. Waterman, IN SEARCH OF EXCELLENCE, Warner Books, Inc., New York, NY.

Philip B. Crosby, QUALITY IS FREE, New American Library, New York, NY.

FORTUNE, Marshall Loeb, Editor, James B. Hayes, Publisher, New York, NY.

MODERN MATERIALS HANDLING, Ray Kulwiec, Editor; William G. Sbordon, Publisher; Cahners Publishing Co., Newton, MA.

INDEX